WHAT SOUTHERN WOMEN KNOW ABOUT FAITH

I truly believe in the power of prayer, and I have lived my whole life on faith. This book speaks to my heart.

DOLLY PARTON

I have no doubt that I am alive and well today due to the fervent prayers of some wonderful Southern women. Ronda, beautifully and entertainingly, tells stories of the kind of Southern women I know. Their faith is the guiding force in their lives, and they discuss it all, and I mean it all, with their Heavenly Father. Like me, I think he too is a softie for a Southern accent.

JEFF FOXWORTHY

Faith is certainly not particular to Southern women, but a few of its revelations and reverberations are. With her right-smack-on voice and sensitivities, Ronda Rich can tell you much about the heart of the Southern woman, and why her faith is such a buoyant and living force in her life.

ANNE RIVERS SIDDONS,
New York Times bestselling author

Y'all, it's amazing how far faith and prayer can carry you. The Serenity Prayer carried this Southern woman to where I am today. This book is a beautiful and inspiring example of Southern women and their faith.

PAULA DEEN

What Southern Women Know about Faith is the kind of book you'll want to give every woman, and man, on your gift list! It is chock-full of the insights and truths about life that simply must be shared.

CASSANDRA KING,
New York Times bestselling author, *The Sunday Wife*

Using her humor, wit, and wisdom, Ronda Rich depicts perfectly what it means to be a Southern woman of strength, softness, and faith.

MARSHA BARBOUR,
First Lady of Mississippi

WHAT
SOUTHERN WOMEN
KNOW ABOUT
FAITH

Also by Ronda Rich

WHAT
SOUTHERN WOMEN
KNOW ABOUT
*F*AITH

Kitchen
Table Stories
and Back Porch
Comfort

RONDA RICH

Foreword by Stevie Waltrip

ZONDERVAN®

ZONDERVAN.com/
AUTHORTRACKER
follow your favorite authors

ZONDERVAN

What Southern Women Know about Faith
Copyright © 2009 by Ronda Rich

This title is also available as a Zondervan ebook.
Visit www.zondervan.com/ebooks.

This title is also available in a Zondervan audio edition.
Visit www.zondervan.fm.

Requests for information should be addressed to:

Zondervan, *Grand Rapids, Michigan 49530*

This edition: ISBN 978-0-310-29186-2 (softcover)

Library of Congress Cataloging-in-Publication Data

Rich, Ronda.
    What Southern women know about faith : kitchen table stories and back porch
comfort / Ronda Rich ; foreword by Stevie Waltrip.
        p.   cm.
    ISBN 978-0-310-29179-4 (hardcover)
    1. Christian women—Southern States—Religious life. I. Title.
BV4527.R54   2009
248.8'43—dc22   2008054081

Scripture quotations are the author's paraphrase based on the King James Version of the
Bible.

Any Internet addresses (websites, blogs, etc.) and telephone numbers printed in this book
are offered as a resource. They are not intended in any way to be or imply an endorsement
by Zondervan, nor does Zondervan vouch for the content of these sites and numbers for
the life of this book.

Interior design: Beth Shagene

Printed in the United States of America

10 11 12 13 14 15 16 • 24 23 22 21 20 19 18 17 16 15 14 13 12 11 10 9 8 7 6 5 4 3 2 1

For Mama—
whose deep and abiding faith carried her through this life
and, most importantly, into life everlasting.

Contents

A NOTE FROM FORMER U.S. SENATOR ZELL MILLER

When I agreed to write a comment about my friend Ronda's new book, I did so because I love and respect this spunky mountain neighbor and have long read everything she writes.

Little did I realize, however, just how deep this farmer's daughter had plowed with this heartwarming, soul-grabbing testimony of her faith and the faith of other Southern women she has known.

It is a marvelous book — an extraordinary book — filled with modern-day parables and the moral lessons to be learned from them. She has taken God's most precious gift, His love, and passed it on to us in a readable and profound way.

I read one story after another, stopping frequently to savor a particular passage that had penetrated my heart so deeply I felt I was there sharing it with her. "My heart was strangely warmed," as John Wesley put it.

This book will take you to the mountaintop with lessons learned from her mother, her father, her family, friends, and race drivers. It is filled with lessons about birth, death, love, and prayer, all told in that straight, soft but steely way that only Ronda can write.

This book will draw you closer to the Lord. It will tickle your funny bone; it will pull at your heart. And it will bring you to your knees. It is that good.

ZELL MILLER, Former U.S. Senator

Foreword
by Stevie Waltrip

My mother's been gone now going on nine years, but I can still hear her sweet voice saying that if I got to the end of my life and could count on just one hand five true friendships, then I would have been truly blessed. If I got to the end of my life and had only one friend and it was Ronda Rich, I would, indeed, be truly blessed.

> Two are better than one,
>> because they have a good return for their work:
> If one falls down,
>> his friend can help him up.
> But pity the man who falls
>> and has no one to help him up!
> Also, if two lie down together, they will keep warm.
>> But how can one keep warm alone?
> Though one may be overpowered,
>> two can defend themselves.
> A cord of three strands is not quickly broken.
>> *Ecclesiastes 4:9–12*

Because of Ronda's faith and her commitment to Jesus Christ, which I have personally witnessed throughout the twenty-plus years that I have known her, I have seen the good return on our work. I have "fallen" in my doubts and unbelief, and have been helped up by Ronda through prayer and encouraging reminders of what the Scriptures say. There have been many times when we have called on each other to pray for family, friends, political issues, cats, dogs—the list goes on and on. Nothing is too insignificant for prayer as far as we are concerned. Upon hearing that I was going to miss my one and only nephew's wedding in Italy because I didn't want to travel alone with two small children (D.W. was working in the broadcast booth for the races), she prayed about it then dropped everything and went with me.

"It's a good thing I came with you," she said many times on that sweet, memorable trip. "Otherwise you'd be lost without me!"

Yes, I would. In more ways and more days than one.

This friendship, like all good, durable friendships, has stood strong during all the days that were tinged with either joy or sorrow. We have grieved together over the loss of our parents, cried over beloved pets that died, laughed over the triumphs of life, and celebrated happily in Victory Lane.

We still talk often about the 1989 Daytona 500. I was in the Tide #17 pits with Ronda. Both of us were working, but just having her alongside me during one of the most high-anxiety races of my and Darrell's lives was truly a gift. She has a contagious positive energy that I always find very comforting and soothing. I knew I could rely on her to pray, and she would not become hysterical if something happened on the track, nor would she ask questions like "Do you think he's going to win?" or make comments like "I think he's going to win." This was no time to talk but just pray because D.W. was trying, for the seventeenth time, to win the 500! She was there for me on that unforgettable day. Thank God!

A year later, she was there for me again. During the last practice of the 1990 Firecracker 400, Darrell was involved in a multi-car crash and was taken to the Halifax Hospital, suffering from a compound fracture of his left femur, broken left arm, several broken ribs, and a concussion. For the first time in his career, he was going to be on the sidelines for several months recovering from these painful injuries.

I was alone in Daytona with my almost three-year-old Jessica, and it was a trying situation. I had a husband and a baby who both needed me. I was waiting for my precious, broken up, incoherent husband to wake up from his six-hour surgery when around the corner at six o'clock in the morning comes my dear friend Ronda. Thank God! Praise Jesus! She'd heard about Darrell's accident on the news at nine o'clock the night of the accident, packed her bags, and headed to Daytona. I couldn't believe my eyes when I saw her. We hadn't talked, so she had no way of knowing how alone I really was. She just listened to her heart and the voice of the Lord. A close friend, you see, always knows when she is needed. She doesn't have to ask.

Despite the time, inconvenience, and all the unknowns, she was there to keep me company, give me strength, and help with Jessica. She's always been there for me. She lets her "light so shine before men, that they may see [her] good works and praise [her] Father in heaven" (Matthew 5:16).

Have you ever longed or prayed for something with all of your heart for many years, yet the Lord denied your request? That's the way it was for Darrell and me when it came to starting a family. We longed desperately for children, and finally after years of trying (we'd been married fifteen years) and a miscarriage, we got pregnant! We were beside ourselves with joy! Four months into that pregnancy, we lost our second baby. We grieved deeply, but we didn't give up hope. In spite of all the reasons medically speaking that we weren't supposed to be able to have kids, and the fact that the clock was ticking away, we prayed together and felt the Lord was telling us to not give up.

We decided against all means of manipulation, opened our hands with our request for a baby, then left the results to Him. Two years later another baby was on the way. Darrell was a nervous wreck with fear and worry. I, on the other hand, was completely confident that everything was going to be all right. Romans 4:18, 20, and 21 says,

> Abraham in hope believed . . . he did not waver through un-
> belief regarding the promise of God, but was strengthened
> in his faith and gave glory to God, being fully persuaded
> that God had power to do what he had promised.

By the grace of God, that is where I stood. On September 17, 1987, Jessica Lee was born to two very undeserving but very grateful people. As I write this, I weep. His mercy and exceedingly abundant grace will always be precious to me. I feel so unworthy yet so thankful.

Not long after Jessica was born I felt that the Lord was telling me He had another baby He wanted to give us. No audible voice, just a strong sense in my spirit. I picked my time carefully to tell Darrell about this divine revelation, but it really did no good. He just stared at me with his mouth gaping as if I'd spoken in Swahili. Once he got his breath back and regained his tongue, he asked me if I'd lost my mind. He then reminded me of the long list of reasons why this wasn't a good idea: We already had a perfectly healthy and normal baby girl, and why would we put ourselves through the risk and grief of losing another baby? How could I even entertain such an idea? He was passionately opposed to the whole idea to put it mildly, but I pressed on and quietly suggested that we pray together and ask the Lord to get us to a point of agreement. We asked Him to change either my heart or Darrell's. He changed Darrell's.

As before, we did nothing to manipulate or control the natural process. We prayed often leaving the results in the Lord's hands.

I was now forty-one years old. Darrell was forty-four. Darrell by now was convinced that I had misunderstood what the Lord had said, and I was even beginning to think that he was right. Time was running out. Age-wise, it was a stretch when we had Jessica. Look at us now!

The year was winding down. It was November, and we were racing in the last race of the 1991 NASCAR season in Atlanta. My dear friend Ronda and I made plans to get together and have lunch at the hotel where we were staying so that we could visit and she could see Jessica.

We spent the day together and ended up in my room so that Jessica could take a nap. I mentioned to her our desire to have another baby and that I had almost given up hope, not quite but almost. Ronda listened intently, becoming aware of how deeply we wanted another baby. In true Ronda form she grabbed my hand and said, "Let's pray!" We got down on our knees in front of that black leather sofa and simply asked the Lord to please give Darrell and me another baby, reminding Him and ourselves of how gracious and kind He is no matter what. We again asked that His will be done and to give Darrell and me the faith and trust that would reflect our love for Him.

The Lord used Ronda's faith and enthusiasm to encourage me. How personal and caring a God is that? He always supplies our needs and sometimes our wants. A little over nine months later (I was forty-two and D.W. was forty-five) we gave birth to another beautiful girl, the completer of our family. We had been married for twenty-three years. Can you beat that? I still marvel at those numbers and God's perfect timing.

Though we never know the Lord's plans, He used that birth to remind us all of how vivid and alive He is and how He resides in the details of our lives. There is another story, a very important one, we all love to tell. Six weeks after we prayed together that day, I called Ronda to tell her the good news. As she told us, a few days later the Lord spoke strongly and almost audibly to her. The revelation was so clear that it was unsettling for Ronda. The baby would be a girl, and she should be named Sarah. "I want that baby named Sarah" were the words Ronda heard ringing in her ears.

Hesitantly, she called and told me. I confess I didn't take it seriously even after a later sonogram confirmed that I was, indeed, carrying a precious baby girl. For the entire pregnancy, Darrell and I debated names and could not come to agreement. Two days before I was scheduled to deliver, we still didn't have a name. Ronda called again.

"Okay, this is none of my business, but the Lord will not leave me alone," she said. "Finally, I told Him that I would call you again and tell you to name that baby Sarah. Now, you do what you want because it's up to you. I'm just telling you again what He told me. If you don't want to listen, *you* can deal with Him. I'm out of it now. I have carried forth my work for the Lord."

She said it comically because she can be very entertaining in her delivery, but there was a strong sincerity that I could not mistake. Something in my spirit stirred.

"Okay," I said this time, "I'll tell you what I'll do: I haven't mentioned to Darrell about your other call, and we have never talked about the name Sarah. I'll ask him to pray about it between now and then and see if any name comes to him. How's that?"

"Wonderful!" Ronda exclaimed. She knew she was off the hook then and it was all up to us and God. I did just as I promised, and Darrell quickly agreed to take it to the Lord in prayer. On the day the baby was born, I held that precious life in my arms, and my husband and I cried together over the gracious mercy of our loving Father.

"We have to name this beautiful girl," I said. "Have you been praying about it?"

"Yes, I have," Darrell replied. "And, Stevie, it is the strangest thing. I keep thinking of one name and one name only. It's one we've never discussed."

"What is it?" I asked as I stared down at the miracle in my arms.

"I keep thinking we should name her Sarah."

I cannot adequately express the feeling that swept over me at that moment. I started crying and said, "Yes, I think we should name her Sarah." When I told him the story of Ronda's phone calls, he broke down and cried too. We knew that the Lord had revealed Himself to all of us in an amazing, real way.

Later that afternoon, Darrell was walking in the door at our home, and the phone was ringing. When he answered it, it was another close friend of mine who, too, had been in serious prayer over the name of our baby.

"Darrell, I've been trying to reach you," Susan said urgently. "Have you named the baby yet?"

"Yes, we have."

"Oh no," she responded. "I've been praying since yesterday over what to name the baby and there is a name that comes to me so strongly, so persistently."

"What is it?" he asked.

"Sarah Kaitlyn."

A few hours earlier, we had named our beautiful new baby, Sarah Kaitlyn Kearns Waltrip.

Darrell, Ronda, or I can never tell this story without tearing up, for we all feel so privileged yet humbled to have watched the hand of God so clearly at work.

> *In his heart a man plans his course,*
> *but the LORD determines his steps.*
> Proverbs 16:9

Darrell and I look back at this time in our lives convinced that God was transforming us to a deeper understanding of who He is, by withholding, taking away, withholding again, and then by His grace, giving and guiding. I am also convinced that this process was very necessary, and I wouldn't take anything for any part of our story to be different.

I think back often to my mother's words about five close friends. As I grow older and, hopefully, wiser, I realize that one of life's truest treasures is friends who love you enough to pray for you. There is no greater love or finer gift than that. I have seen repeatedly the compassion, care, and prayers that Ronda had for me as we watched the gentle warm hand of God work.

Also, I am blessed to have another close friend who loves me powerfully despite my flaws and short comings, who knows what I stand in need of before I know it, and who, as the Scriptures say, knows my "downsitting and mine uprising." As the old gospel hymn says so well, "What a friend we have in Jesus."

I smile as I think of my sweet Lord and my precious Ronda. I have a dear friend on earth who prays for me and another in Heaven who hears and answers those prayers.

What a beloved blessing.

INTRODUCTION

On most mornings of my younger life, I would awake to the delicious aroma of sizzling bacon drifting in from the red-and-white tile-floor kitchen where Mama was up, bright and early, making a big breakfast. The smells, sights, and sounds of those big Southern breakfasts are still vivid in my mind: hot bacon or sausage grease popping loudly and escaping from the black cast-iron skillet, the coffee pot whistling, sawmill gravy boiling to a creamy thickness, steam rising up from fluffy handmade buttermilk biscuits, grits simmering in the well-worn, battered boiler, and broken egg shells scattered across the countertop next to the stove. She poured Daddy's coffee, added sugar and cream, and then called, "It's ready."

Mama had a penchant for mashing butter into her scrambled eggs with a fork and then adding extra pepper. As she did so, and as Daddy sipped his coffee before starting his own breakfast, they would inevitably begin a morning conversation about the trials and tribulations faced by either our family or those we knew. For both, their first awakening action had been to pray silently to our good Lord Almighty.

Daddy would then throw his long legs off the bed, lean forward to put his elbows on his knees, and talk it all over with the Lord until Mama called him to breakfast.

Most of those morning conversations around the kitchen table would include phrases such as "The good Lord will answer in his own time," "We'll just have to leave it in God's hands. He knows better than us," "We can't question God, we just have to trust," "The Lord won't let us down," "We'll just take these troubles to the Lord in prayer and leave them there," "God has it all in the palm of his mighty hand," and "We just have to have faith. It'll all work out. Don't worry."

As bacon was munched, coffee sipped, and biscuits pushed around the plates to sop up the last dredges of gravy, worries seemed to melt away with a vivid, vibrant faith reaffirmed through both word and action. There around that old oval-shaped oak table, I first learned of the faith of my people, the kind of faith that I have repeatedly witnessed over the years across the South of my upbringing. It is a faith that is plain, simple, and sturdy, that is utilitarian in practice and fits as comfortably in the hands of Southern women as a baby, an iron skillet, a hairbrush, a telephone, a book, or a broom.

It's best described as a kitchen-table faith because it sits comfortably in our midst like a lifelong trusted neighbor who is always there at our beck and call, who enters through the kitchen door and stays a spell. It is a faith that does not require us to dress in our Sunday best, assemble in the church house, or make an appointment at the altar in order to find it. Nor is it a faith to which we only subscribe to and feed on Sundays. It is faith that undergirds us every morning, afternoon, and evening of our lives.

Our faith, as practiced by the Southern women I know, walks beside us minute by minute, with its arms slung casually and sweetly around our shoulders, ready to embrace us tightly when the trials and heartaches of this life make rocky the road that we walk. When we stumble, as we all do from time to time, that ever-present faith grabs an elbow and steadies us on the uneven path.

"Wherever you are, God is there," Mama always said. "He'll meet you wherever you are."

On Sundays, my sister, Louise, will cook a huge dinner for our family and serve it piping hot after church ends. Twelve or so adults and children will pile into the big open kitchen that spills into a sun-kissed dining area and family room. After the blessing is said, the mashed potatoes, green beans, and fried chicken are passed, and the sweet tea is poured. Forks will clink against the pottery, and talk will inevitably turn to that morning's Sunday school lesson or sermon, and a theological discussion will ensue or a recent experience of God's grace will be shared. Most of the table time will be spent discussing faith, both the pragmatic and the practiced. Just as in the early days of my life, the faith of my family still rises up bountifully from the kitchen table.

One day I stood in the dairy aisle of a small grocery store in a tiny town in rural Tennessee. As I selected a carton of milk, my ears tuned into the conversation of two women standing behind me, their grocery carts parked beside each other. One's voice was filled with sadness as she explained her medical concerns for her son. The other's voice was filled with sincere compassion as she gently said, "I'll be praying for you. With God, all things are possible."

I smiled to myself, warmed by a faith that is ever present among our women whether they reside in Tennessee, the Carolinas, Georgia, Mississippi, Alabama, Arkansas, Louisiana, Kentucky, Virginia, Texas, or have transplanted and sowed their seeds of faith and belief in other places. In a grocery store in the middle of nowhere in

Tennessee, I had witnessed the same kind of faith that I encounter every day in my homeland: a biblically based trust that is buried deep in our hearts and discussed comfortably among each other at a moment's notice.

Does the faith of Southern women impress God more than others? Certainly not. Does the faith of Southern women offer redemption or salvation more than others? Absolutely not. But what is different about it—and why this book now exists—is the steady, consistent way that it is practiced among our women. Our society is so deeply entrenched in an active, engaged faith that rarely will a conversation of any length between two Southern women not allude to or outright mention spirituality. Our culture is saturated with religious conviction, soaked completely to the bone with it.

These days, I spend much of my time with the good Lord out on my sprawling back porch as I read my Bible, study the writings of scholars, pray, and reflectively seek his guidance and wisdom. I find solace in my favorite rocker or in that sweet white porch swing, where I am surrounded by the wonder of God's creation in the form of towering hardwood trees, squirrels that jump playfully from limb to limb, and a nearby tiny river that ebbs slowly by on its way to meet the ocean somewhere. That rippling water is a subtle reminder that little things often lead to bigger things in the divine plan of our heavenly Father. In the rural North Georgia countryside, it isn't a large amount of water, but one day it will join an almost endless ocean and be part of something much bigger. So is, I believe, the Lord's plan for my life. It is small in presence, but it is meant to be part of a bigger, grander plan.

On the quiet back porch, I often crawl figuratively into the lap of my heavenly Father, just as I once did with my earthly father, to seek comfort, love, and guidance. Just as the Lord was always waiting for us each morning at the kitchen table of my childhood, I find him waiting on the back porch whenever I need a reprieve from the harshness and uncertainty of life or when I want to praise and thank him for the mighty blessings that so often fall on my life and the lives of those I love.

My only wish as you embark on this reading journey is that you will snatch pieces of joy and comfort hither and yon, and that when all is said and done, this little book will find its humble place in God's bigger, grander plan.

Chapter 1

THERE'S POWER IN THE BLOOD

Out of the poverty-stricken foothills of the Southern Appalachian mountains come my people. Many of them Scotch-Irish, some of them English. For over two hundred years, they traipsed through those beautiful laurel-covered mountains in the form of farmers, mule traders, moonshiners, mothers, Sunday school teachers, in-laws, out-laws, fiddle players, storytellers, and preachers.

They make up an interesting culture, these Southern Appalachians, for they are a goodly mix of the righteous and the renegades who often warred against each other. In generations past, and perhaps even some today, there were those who loved the Lord with all their hearts and those who ran from him with all their might. It always seemed that sooner or later, the good Lord would catch up with the renegades, bringing the righteous to say, "There comes a day of reckonin'. There always does."

I descend from many generations of God-fearing, Jesus-loving, fervent-praying people. People of strong and immeasurable faith. When my first Scotch-Irish ancestors came to America in the mid-1700s, they were Presbyterian, but as they moved further down the Appalachians to western North Carolina and northern Georgia, they were forced to turn Baptist.

You see, the Presbyterians ordain only scholarly, well-educated men for their pulpits. That was a problem for two reasons. First, they couldn't turn them out of divinity school fast enough to supply the exploding population of the Southern mountains, and secondly, these refined men didn't always cotton to the primitive backwoods life; so finding the willing in spirit as well as in body to go forth among the less civilized proved a bit hard for the Presbyterian church.

The Baptists, though, are surprisingly more liberal. At least in this aspect. To be ordained for a Baptist pulpit simply meant, and still means, that a man must have the calling of the Holy Spirit on his life, and, therefore, laymen — farmers and the like — could and did pastor churches.

"The Lord called him," folks would say one to another about a man who had publicly announced his calling by the Spirit to preach. "How 'bout that? He made a preacher." "Making a preacher," in the vernacular of our people, was what they viewed as the highest calling and most prestigious honor in humble mountain life. Much grander than that even of making a doctor.

Beginning in the early 1800s, the Presbyterians became Baptists and the Baptists became rulers of those mountains. It would grow to be the largest Protestant denomination in America, while the South and its ever-faithful flock would become the unyielding heart of America's Bible Belt.

The faith of my people has always been simple. We have always believed in a benevolent God who hears and answers prayers. When my ancestors fell on their knees to pray, they prayed with a fervency that could rock those mighty mountains. No, the good Lord does not always answer as we see fit. He does not always answer as we have prayed he will. But he always answers according to his will, and sometimes his will and ours are sweetly the same.

My people have clung faithfully to the King James Version of the Bible, spouting its lyrical words from memory and knowing Scripture to fit every heartache, joy, or need. We have worshiped the Almighty from the simple structures of white clapboard country churches with gravel paths leading to them, sung praises with old-fashioned hymns accompanied by ancient upright pianos with yellowed keys, baptized the redeemed in clear, rushing rivers, and buried our dead in cemeteries behind those simple churches.

I descend directly from some of those Spirit-called foot soldiers in the battlefield for the Lord. Paw-paw, my mother's father, was a humble man of no financial means, but he preached salvation throughout the Nimblewill Valley, outside of Dahlonega, Georgia. He and my grandmother were instrumental in bringing my daddy, a scion of the renegades, into the righteous fold. Though he would spend a couple of years running from the call of the Lord, he did finally succumb and would become one of the most revered preachers in the North Georgia mountains.

Until I was seven years old, Daddy pastored two churches at one time, not an unusual practice in those days. One church — Town Creek — met for worship on the first and third Sundays, while the other — Tesnatee — held meetings on the second and fourth Sundays in a little white clapboard church perched on a picturesque hill. The occasional fifth Sunday was spent visiting or preaching at other churches. When Tesnatee decided it had a large enough congregation, Daddy became pastor of one church. I was eight years old. He always preached only for love offerings, which were never very much. Once a full week's revival had yielded only seven dollars in the collection plate to share between two preachers. Daddy gave the full bounty to the other preacher.

"I preach for the Lord, not for money," he would often say. Our family was supported by the money he made in his garage from repairing cars—another layman turned preacher.

In Deuteronomy the Scripture commands believers to tithe from their fields and crops. In those days so many years ago, both Paw-paw and Daddy found that while their humble congregations could not line their pockets with coins, they could certainly laden their tables with food. So they were paid in tithes of turnips, cornmeal ground in the nearby mills powered by the mighty rivers, corn, tomatoes, green beans, a bounty of other fruits and vegetables, fresh eggs, and live chickens.

Once an old man in Daddy's congregation, who dressed regularly in overalls and an old work shirt for church, stopped to shake Daddy's hand on his way out the door after service.

"Preacher, if'n you would, stop by my place on yer way home." The man with hands hardened by work in the field, pulled an old handkerchief from his pocket and wiped a bit of snuff from the corner of his mouth. "Got somethin' I wanna give ya."

When Daddy arrived, the old man motioned for him to follow, hobbled out to the barn, then stopped at the hog pen. Several small piglets played in the mud close to their mama.

"Pick ya a pig," the man said proudly, smiling at what was the greatest gift he could give. "Pick any one of 'em you want. That'un over there's a good 'un. Gonna make a huge hog and give ya plenty of meat to feed that family of your'un."

"Now, Brother Jarrard, you don't have to do that," Daddy protested, knowing the man barely could make ends meet.

The man's eyes watered. "Preacher, I ain't got no money to give ya, so I wanna give ya what I got to give. I aim to pay my way in this church, same as everybody else."

In the corner of the pen was a tiny runt, half the size of its siblings. Daddy pointed to him. "Then I'll take that one."

The old man's eyes widened, and he shook his head vigorously. "No, no, no. That'un's the runt. Ain't much good for nothin'. You take the best 'un in there you kin find."

Daddy tilted his head, put his hands on his hips and reminded him, "You said I could have whichever one I want, and that's the one I want. You ain't goin' back on your word now, are you?"

The man, prouder of his word than anything else, as were all of his kind, sighed heavily, caught the tiny creature, put it in an old feed sack, and sent it home with the preacher. Daddy, knowing that the old farmer could make more money and produce more food from the healthier pigs, had chosen the least. But the least would become great, growing into an enormous hog that Daddy later slaughtered and then filled Mama's old freezer with dozens of packages of sausage, roast, bacon, and pork loin. He would use every ounce of that hog, turning its fat into lard for cooking and producing cracklins to spiff up an ordinary cake of cornbread.

The greatest prayer warrior I have ever known was my daddy. From him I learned to pray. He prayed earnestly with his words crackling in voice-choking humility. And though he has been gone for years now, I can still hear clearly the words with which he ended every prayer, "Dear Lord, we bow our unworthy heads and give you the honor, the praise, and the glory for it all. Amen."

Those people who came before me never prayed for more than

what they needed. No one ever prayed for fame, riches, or earthly glory. That, they all believed, was waiting on the other side of the River Jordan. They prayed simply for what it would take to survive this life until they could make it to the other side. When death came, illness plagued, the skies didn't rain and the crops died, or taxes were to be paid, my people had found one Scripture buried in the Old Testament that would become their mantra. From one to another, they would pass it when encouragement was needed and despair had to be shed.

"Remember what David said," one would remind the other. " 'I once was young and now I'm old, yet I have never seen the righteous forsaken or his seed begging bread.' "

Prayer and faith lie at the center of my family. On the early November night that the Lord called Daddy home, my mama, siblings, and other loved ones had gathered around that which had been my parents' marriage bed for over fifty years and prayed. We prayed first that Daddy wouldn't linger in the coma that the massive stroke had wrought early that morning. When that prayer was answered many hours later, as the enormous Hunter's full moon hung boldly in the dark sky outside the bedroom window, we prayed again, thanking God for his mercy and for the life of a faithful servant that had touched so many. Like his hero, the apostle Paul, he too had fought a good fight and finished the course. Then we sang "Amazing Grace" and one verse of "I'll Fly Away." Though we have always known the comfort and peace that prayer through our faith can bring, we knew it in abundance on that fateful day.

The Bible says to pray without ceasing, and sometimes I believe I do just that. I wander through my house doing mundane things, such as sweeping the floor or loading the dishwasher, while I have chats with God. I find myself looking for a misplaced file in my office and mumble, "Now, Lord, where is *that*? Please help me find it." And moments later, I will put my hands on it in some odd place and immediately whisper with a bit of a laugh, "Thank you, Lord. I knew you knew where it was."

I pray for simple things. Yes, I have prayed for a parking place in an overcrowded lot at the mall. And found one of the best. I have prayed that a lost package would be found by the post office. And it was. I have prayed that my car would make it to a gas station in the dark of night in the middle of nowhere. And it has.

I have prayed for profound things. Or so they seemed at the time. I have prayed that a guy who I adored would love me. But he never did. I have prayed for a job that I thought was perfect and would utterly complete my life. But I didn't get it. Yet through those unanswered prayers, I discovered that God's plan for my life was grander and much smarter than I would have ever thought of asking. I have finally learned that when he answers no to my prayers, I will profit more than if he had answered yes.

I have prayed for things that seem insignificant but I believed could yield either significant results or dire consequences. Before every speaking engagement, I pray that my mind will conjure up the right words and touch the hearts of those who hear me with either laughter or inspiration. Before I write, I pray for guidance, knowing that I am an empty vessel until a divine Spirit deems me worthy to be filled with creative inspiration. Before difficult conversations I pray that my words will be effective and not harmful or hurtful.

I have prayed fervently to calm the tidal wave of sorrow roaring toward me, begging God to still the waters of sadness over the impending homegoing of loved ones, who were being beckoned by heaven but I couldn't bear for them to leave this earth. Sometimes he has answered and given me my heart's desire. Sometimes he hasn't.

There was that boy, my childhood nemesis, who slammed me in the eye with a baseball bat at eight, tried to drown me at eleven, but who grew handsome and strong and won my heart completely when I was fifteen. In one way or the other, it seemed I had loved him all my life. I was in New Orleans on book tour when the heart-shredding news came by phone from Mama. Pancreatic cancer, she said. Not much time.

Months before Katrina flooded the streets of that city, I had walked its sidewalks and flooded them with my own tears, prayerfully beseeching God for a miracle. I wouldn't accept death as the answer. I believed that I could pray him well. I seized upon the Scripture that says, "Wherever two are in agreement of anything touching on earth, it shall be done for them in heaven."

I called my closest friend, Karen, a Grammy-nominated gospel singer. "Every day, we shall pray together on the phone, and we'll pray him well." Six weeks came, the time when the doctor said he would be dead. But he wasn't. He was alive and, amazingly, the cancer had retreated. Within a few months, it looked as if he had defied the odds. I prayed and thanked God for that reprieve. But that's what it was—only a reprieve. Death had been delayed but refused to be deterred.

On the day before the Lord called him home, Karen and I visited him together. His body was ravaged with uninterrupted pain, and those who loved him mightily could not bear to see him suffer. The time had come to pray that God would ease his pain—even if it brought to the rest of us unbearable sorrow.

In her pitch-perfect voice, Karen sang "Amazing Grace" a cappella. Then, I did the only thing I knew would bring comfort to his wearied soul as death plucked persistently in his ear. I prayed. I knelt, taking his bony, frail hand in mine — the previously strong one I had held so many times over the years — and in a voice tinged in sorrow, I called on Almighty God to help us all. I do not recall one word I said, for the words rose up naturally from my broken heart and somehow managed to get around the knot in my throat to escape my lips. Though I don't remember one word, I shall never forget how our tears fell like icy droplets on our joined hands. Or how the moment I whispered, "Amen," he turned his world weary eyes to mine and mumbled softly, "Thank you."

For even as death eased closer and we had to accept that our previous prayers for healing would not be answered, we still found comfort in the presence of the Lord through prayer and faith.

Though he hasn't always answered my prayers in the way I wanted, or even sometimes demanded, he is still a great and mighty God to me just as he was to my ancestors. From those quaint and odd Scotch-Irish I have inherited much — red hair, stubbornness, a gift for storytelling, an independence of spirit that isn't always pretty, a strong work ethic, and an unyielding belief in the power of prayer and the faith in a higher power that sustains me. I have also inherited a legacy that man cannot put asunder and that is the finest heirloom that can pass from one generation to another.

For this I know: prayer and faith always work. One way or the other.

Chapter 2

SOUTHERN SUNDAYS

For whatever reason, summer always reminds me most of the precious Sundays of my childhood. As trees green up, flowers bloom, and weather warms, I am always, without fail, drawn back to a time when the weekly worship of the Lord was sacred, family was gathered together without fail, and Southern cooking was spread with exceeding abundance on the dinner table.

Though all of these were important every Sunday of the year, summer Sundays were special, kicked off on Easter and lasting through Labor Day. Every Easter, I had a completely new outfit, right down to my socks and lace-trimmed bloomers. What a woman wears on Easter in the South is of enormous importance.

"Have you got your Easter outfit yet?" women will ask one another for weeks leading up to the celebration of Christ's victory over death. To this day, it is the bane of my existence—finding the right hat and outfit for the big day of celebration. It may not be perfectly and humbly Christian, but I do try to outdo the other women with my attire. In my family we even have an Easter parade after church in which each person walks out the door onto the front porch, waves at my brother-in-law, Rodney, who is filming it while adding both necessary and unnecessary commentary, then sashays down the steps, and walks up the sidewalk out of view. It is an austere tradition, envied by many.

"How did we get started with this tradition of new clothes on Easter?" I asked a friend.

"It signifies the beginning of all things new," she responded authoritatively. "Christ died on Good Friday and arose on Easter, so that signified the dawning of the new Day of Grace. No longer were we shackled to the Law. It was a new day. That's why we have new clothes to wear on Easter Sunday."

I think she made all that up, but it sounds good, so I'll just go with it too. After all, the Bible has a lot of symbols, so we'll just let new clothes — at least in the South — be symbolic of a new life under the Day of Grace. Anyway, once Easter came, Sundays were rife with new meaning and excited new purpose. Folks took to standing out in the churchyard and talking longer while children ran and played merrily in youthful fellowship. To me, that's one of the truest signs of a strong, loving church family — one that will gather outside after service and fellowship.

One Sunday after early church not long ago, I had to run out to my car before Sunday school. As I scurried down the steps, I noticed a few small groups of people laughing and talking in the churchyard. I hurried by a group of men and heard one say, "Did you see who's on the pole for the race today? I couldn't believe my ears when I heard it."

"I have a new recipe for strawberry cake that you've got to try," one woman was saying to another as I passed them by.

"I got me a problem with my ol' tractor that I can't rightly figure out," a man of grayed age was saying to a younger one. "I's wonderin' if you could take a look at it and tell me what you think the problem is."

As I opened the door of my car, I smiled, thinking of neighbors worshiping together and enjoying each other. Jesus, I believe, is pleased with that. After 11 a.m. church, people will often stand and talk for half an hour or so before they saunter on home.

In the days of my childhood, church folks often took the preacher and his family home for dinner. By the way, in the rural South, big lunches, especially those on Sunday, are called dinner. It was the folks' way of helping to pay the preacher. That seldom happens anymore, and I do hate to see that pass to the wayside. One Sunday night after church, my sister, brother-in-law, and I joined the preacher and his wife for a hamburger down at the diner.

"Do people ever take y'all home for dinner any more on Sundays?" I asked, guilty as anyone of not asking and cooking.

Wistfully, both smiled and shook their gray heads, for their age was enough that they remembered that bountiful time not all that long ago.

"Hardly ever happens," the preacher said sadly, not, I am certain, because he needed the meal but because it allowed him to spend less one-on-one time with his flock.

Driving home that night, I thought back to those hundreds of Sundays when various members of the congregation had taken my preacher daddy, Mama, and me home for dinner. What a treat that usually was. Miss Cora and Mr. Harrison asked us often, and it was always the most delicious meal — with succulent roast beef, fried chicken, mashed potatoes, gravy, corn, fresh green beans, homemade biscuits, and delicious cobblers, pies, and cakes.

Mr. Harrison Nix was a well-to-do landowner, but he and Miss Cora lived in a simple five-room white clapboard house with a screen porch on the front. We'd eat in their tiny dining room on an old hand-hewn table, with Daddy and Mr. Harrison squeezed in between the wall and the table. Later, we'd sit on the front porch on a pleasant afternoon, and I would listen as the folks exchanged stories. Sometimes, I'd retire my little self to the bedroom and take a nap on the old iron bed, sleeping face down on the chenille bedspread. Whenever I see one of those bedspreads, I smile, thinking back to the days when I'd wake up, look in the antique vanity mirror, and see my face imprinted with the dotted pattern of the white bedspread.

When summer revivals came, some of the church women of great authority, usually self-imposed, would go around to the members and arrange for different families to take the preacher's family home for dinner every day of revival. Without fail, each woman went all out to put the best spread possible out for the preacher, so by the time revival ended, we'd all gained weight, but it was weight enjoyably earned amidst the down-home hospitality of sweet friends.

Of course, up in the mountains, just like down in the towns, you could always count on a certain amount of drama. Like the Sunday in August when we had just finished lunch with one family. The grown-ups sat outside on old kitchen chairs spread under the shade of the enormous oak tree, talking, while I, barely weaned from my Daddy's knee, sprawled on the ground, half-listening, while I flipped through a book. I happened to glance up and saw a woman coming up the road before the rest of them did. I knew it was Gladys. She was in regular attendance at our little country church.

"Looky there," Gladys' mama, our hostess, said in a puzzled voice. The others looked to see Gladys stomping up the red dirt road with a baby straddling her bony hip and trailing a string of straggled-looking young'uns behind her. She was wearing a lightweight cotton dress, flat loafers covered with dry summer dust, and swinging a black pocketbook crooked in one arm. Even I, innocent though I was, could tell she was mad.

"Howdy do," she said politely to us, unsmiling. Then she turned her stony glare to her daddy and mama.

"I come home," she said plaintively, lifting her chin stubbornly. "I've up and left that man, and I ain't a-goin' back. I done made up my mind, and it's gonna stay made up."

It stayed made up, all right. For Gladys moved that passel of young'uns into that tiny white-frame house and stayed put for the rest of her days to come. That man, I overheard the grown-ups talking, had come home drunk one time too many, his pockets empty from another night of poker. Oh, he tried to get her back, throwing his dignity to the wind and carrying on with unbecoming rousts of howling, moaning, and begging. She turned a deaf ear and that was that. I guess that was my first lesson in how a woman can be pushed across the line and never turn back.

A practice in the churches at that time, which still continues to a certain extent these days, was that members referred to each other as "Brother" or "Sister."

"Brother Satterfield, good to have you with us today," a minister might welcome a visitor in the congregation. That, of course, emerges from the Biblical teaching that when we accept Christ, we become part of the family of God, all brothers and sisters through the grace of our Father.

My favorite summer memories, the ones that live the strongest in my heart, are those spent with family after church. We'd all meet up at my grandparents, devour an enormous country meal, nearly all of it homegrown, then while the adults settled down on the front porch in the scattered hand-made rockers, we cousins and our friends would dash off for the swimming hole. There we would frolic, laugh, try to drown each other, and ride inner tubes over the rapids in the river.

When the swimming ended, we'd run back to the house, beg a dollar off our parents, and then, still dripping with the river's water, walk a mile barefooted to the country store to buy candy, ice cream, and Cokes. When the afternoon was over, our souls, those of both the adults and the children, were refreshed and our bodies relaxed. We had spent the day connecting with God, family, and nature. To Southerners, a sense of place is enormously important and often defines who we are, for it tells from where we come. Returning to that family place on a regular basis tucks us securely into the bosom of our lineage and reminds us of those who have come before us and built the foundation of our families.

Louise, my sister, carries on that tradition of family by cooking a big family dinner and loading down the table. Their kids, grandkids, and others like me pile in with an abundance of clatter and chatter. One Sunday, Nix, a first-grader, found a discarded cardboard roll that had once had wrapping paper on it. It became his toy of the day. Nix, who has a vivid imagination, used it as a sword, then a golf club, then a baseball bat, then as a club — a weapon of destruction. All afternoon, he chased the other kids with it and used it to its maximum potential. As he got in the car that day, he said, "Wow! This is the best toy I've ever had in the world!"

We chuckled, of course, and shook our heads because he had so many state-of-the-art toys, but it reminded me of how easy children are to entertain. They don't need an abundance of high-priced toys. Their imaginations can take them on terrific adventures. Out of the trash, Nix had pulled a cardboard roll and created a great adventure with it. Just like we did down at the swimming hole. Or when we made mud pies in old tin pie plates our mamas had thrown out and then left them in the sun to bake.

Unequivocally, the most precious gift you can give your children is to teach them about the Lord and help them find their way to eternal salvation. Also precious, though, is to give them a sense of place and the love of extended family with a lot of good food thrown in. If you take Sundays to focus on faith, family, food, and fun, you will give yourself and those you love the kind of happy, solid memories that will sustain them through unhappy and trying times. It will create the kind of tradition — like our Easter parade — that your children and your children's children will want to carry on through the years.

One Sunday, while visiting friends in Nashville, we had gone to church and then to a restaurant for lunch (it's only dinner when it's home-cooked). As we waited to be seated, others filed in, obviously fresh from church because all the women were dressed so lovely and the men were attired in jackets, suits, and ties. There is still a certain decorum of how we dress for church in the South, though many churches have gone casual. Sadly, no one ever refers to "Sunday clothes" any more — those dresses and suits are reserved only for church, funerals, and weddings — but we still take a lot of pride in how we dress to meet the Lord at his house. That Sunday in Nashville, I watched the handsome parade of well-dressed folks and smiled.

Yes, there's something — or rather *many* things — I like about Sundays in the South. But mostly it's the fellowship that brings people together, while dividing our worries, that delivers a soothing respite for body, mind, and soul. God set the example — he always does, you know — by resting on the seventh day.

Chapter 3

THE CORNBREAD
OF LIFE

*M*ake do or do without," Mama often said as I was growing up. She was merely passing along the philosophy of her childhood. It was one of the instructions of Appalachian life that she had learned solidly. Many times, I have watched Mama make do in astoundingly ingenious ways. Whether it was substituting one recipe ingredient she didn't have on hand for one she did, rigging up curtains without the proper hardware, or turning an odd, misshaped piece of fabric into a lovely dress, she was a master of making do without having to do without.

Mama, with Scotch-Irish blood coursing stubbornly through her veins, had no appreciation for the words "no" or "can't."

"I'll figure out a way to do it," she often said, and she always did.

Mama's faith, coupled with her own resourceful elbow grease, heeded the call of making do time after time. That's typical, for our women have never believed in sitting back and handing it all over to God when there are things we can do to nudge impossibility into probability.

"The good Lord appreciates a helping hand from time to time," Mama would say.

When the hundreds of thousands of Scotch-Irish arrived in those mountains, they brought with them skills that would ultimately define them, including a penchant for creating music, telling stories, and making whiskey. In the rock-hard red dirt of those mountains, few crops would grow. But corn grew and it grew so plentiful that its bounty drove down the market prices. That's how men like my daddy's papa had ended up in the moonshining business.

"Daddy could take a bushel of corn and sell it for fifty cents or he could turn it into a quart of likker that sold for two dollars and a half," my daddy explained to me years later. "When you got mouths to feed and taxes to pay, what would you do?"

Of course, men like that didn't take kindly to men like my other granddaddy telling 'em what to do. They didn't want to be preached at about redemption. Heaven, indeed, might be waiting, but so was the tax man. In the end, though, most of those renegades like Daddy's papa found salvation. But they found it on their own terms—when no one else was bossing them—and in their own, mule-stubborn time.

The corn that grew plentiful there became the main substance for their bodies when they ground it into meal at one of the mills positioned on a river. In the winters particularly, when there were no fresh vegetables and meat was scarce, they sustained themselves on pones of cornbread made from that meal and milk.

The heartiness of that meal would stick with Daddy for the rest of his life. A few times a week, he would bypass whatever else Mama cooked and say, "I'll just have milk and bread." She'd bake a hot pan of cornbread for him, which he then crumbled into a soup bowl and poured buttermilk over it. He loved every crumb as much as if it were a big, juicy steak. In that respect and in others, I am my daddy's daughter. Often when I finish work at the end of the day, I crave hoe-cakes (cornbread fried in patties in a cast iron skillet) and buttermilk. I have it for supper a couple of times a week.

Like many in the Bible, our people often sustained themselves on bread. The manna that God sent to feed the children of Israel each morning and night was bread that fell from heaven. When they complained that they'd rather have meat, he sent meat that they were forced to eat until it ran from their nostrils. After that, they were happy to go back to bread.

When Satan wanted to tempt Jesus during his forty-day fast in the wilderness, he tauntingly told Jesus to turn the rocks into bread, and later, when Jesus needed to feed the multitudes, he multiplied the loaves of bread and fish. Throughout the Bible when there was nothing else to eat, God always provided bread. Knowing that, Jesus warned, "Man shall not live by bread alone, but by every word that proceedeth out of the mouth of God" (Matthew 4:4).

God-fearing Southern women have always taken that Scripture to heart by picking up the word of God with our hands. Bread sustains our earthly bodies, but our souls need nourishment too. Southern women are faithful to our faith and the faith of those who came before us. Each generation passed down Bibles that were well-worn from constant reading and studying. The message is clear as those loved ones speak to us through the silent words of death: Read this book daily.

Interestingly, in the book of John, where Jesus, as an adult, first appears and performs his first miracles, he refers to himself as the bread of life: "I am the bread of life; he that cometh to me shall never hunger; and he that believeth on me shall never thirst" (John 6:35).

Then Jesus pointed out that the children of Israel were given earthly bread to sustain their earthly bodies, but he offered spiritual bread that guarantees everlasting life: "Your fathers did eat manna in the wilderness, and are dead. This is the bread which came down from heaven: if any man eat of this bread, he shall live forever: and the bread that I will give is my flesh, which I will give for the life of the world" (John 6:49–51).

Then Jesus drove home his point, making it abundantly clear: "I am the living bread which cometh down from heaven" (John 6:51).

The analogy is perfect. We cannot survive in this life nor have everlasting life without bread in one form or another. While family and food are enormously important to Southern life, it is the faith of our women that carries us forth. And that faith is undergirded with an uncompromising belief in the Word of God and what it teaches and what it demands of us. Southern women have a high standard for life practices, and that standard is pushed higher by what the Bible instructs. It's hard to turn the other cheek, not seek vengeance, and love those who seek to hurt us. But by striving to do those things, we raise our standards as a person and a Christian.

I don't know about you, but loving — genuinely loving — someone who has deliberately sought to hurt me by stabbing me in the back or outright lying about me, is the hardest thing that I've ever been called upon to do as a Christian. The Bible says to pray for those who despitefully use us, and to be honest, that helps me more than anything in how I feel for them. I humble myself and pray for those I really prefer to dislike vigorously. In fact, I have a funny story about that.

It all started when I got roped into doing a volunteer kindness that involved contact with an arrogant, blustery man who treated me very unkindly. But I learned from it. See, I have discovered in life that mean people can teach us as much as good people. From the good ones, we learn how to behave. From the mean ones, we learn how not to behave.

From the pool of someone else's pettiness, I caught my own reflection. I saw how I must have looked in times past. I was aghast at the ugliness and resolved I didn't want to look or act like that even though I was hurt and upset and wanted to get back at him. I was already struggling with my own conscience when God got involved. I kept unintentionally running into Scriptures about "recompense not evil with evil" and such.

In fact, in my daily Bible reading on the day after he had treated me so ugly, I *accidentally* — which means it was divinely delivered — read Romans 12:17 – 21. The last few lines read: "Vengeance is mine; I will repay saith the Lord. Therefore if thine enemy hunger, feed him; if he thirst, give him drink: for in so doing thou shall heap coals of fire on his head."

Then it ended with this — and this is what got me: "Be not overcome of evil, but overcome evil with good."

Next, my pastor preached that very Sunday on "Love thy enemies and pray for thy offenders." I was getting it every way I turned.

I wasn't much on praying for the villain, but I decided it was the thing to do and started as soon as I left church.

"Did you really?" asked my friend Karen.

I smiled brightly. "Yes, I did. I prayed that he will bite his tongue off so that he will never again be able to speak ugly about anyone or to cause trouble."

She gasped mightily. "You did not pray that! Tell me you didn't."

"Well, I did, but, of course, I prayed that it will be painless when it happens."

We both got a big laugh out of it because she knew I really hadn't prayed that. As hard as it was, I had prayed that his life would be blessed. The end of the story is that we never became friends, but I do continue to pray for him whenever he crosses my mind. At one point, he even came to me and apologized, which I accepted. See, had I refused his apology or sought revenge in any way, my blessings would have been in jeopardy, not his. Plus, in doing as the Bible instructed, I found peace that surpasses all understanding.

Finding a solution to a common problem that many of us face was as easy as picking up my daddy's worn, black Bible that rests on my nightstand. I make it a practice to start each day by reading its wisdom. The ironic thing is that the morning that the good Lord spoke directly to me through his words, I had held the book in my hands and whispered, "Dear Lord, let this book fall open to the Scriptures I need today." It had fallen open to the book of Romans, the twelfth chapter, with its admonishments against retaliation.

That was no accident.

My niece, Nicole, never misses her morning Bible study. I mean never. I, on the other hand, can miss it when I'm running late for the airport or out of town. Nicole, though, carries her Bible everywhere. We can be in New York for a shopping trip, but before we head to Bloomingdale's, she scoots over to a corner of the room and reads her Bible.

For us, the Bible is life's instruction book. Plain and simple. It lays out the path to eternal life and gives us a complete strategic plan for dealing with this life: Ten Commandments, the necessity of faith combined with prayer, tithing, management of grief, dealing with those who dislike us, maintaining humility, and loving those who seem so unlovable.

It is the Bible's ancient truths that have seen countless numbers of Southerners through the rigors of life including strife, trouble, and heartbreak, while teaching us how to graciously deal with success and triumph. We are gently reminded by its words that when we are blessed, it is our responsibility to return a portion of those blessings back to others. Yes, I tithe. It is almost mechanical with me to give back ten percent of my income to the Lord and his people in need. But I also tithe blessings, those wonderful gifts that come along in life with no money attached. A favor that someone has done for me, a kind word when my day is drear, and an unexpected gift are all reasons for tithing a kindness back to someone else.

One day I was standing in line at a big discount store behind a young girl who was buying a DVD with a gift card. The cashier took the card and then told her that she was a dollar short. The young girl searched frantically through her purse and billfold but couldn't find a single cent.

"How much do you need?" I asked them.

"Ninety nine cents," the cashier responded.

"Oh, I've got that. Hang on." So, I pulled out a dollar and paid the rest of the bill. The young girl was grateful and sweetly thanked me before leaving. Silently, I thought to myself, "I hope this is a lesson she takes forward and shares somewhere else down the line."

When the cashier rang up my order, I was trying to find the right change without breaking a bigger bill. I counted my money and laughed.

"I was going to give you the correct change but I'm a dollar short because I just gave her that dollar." I handed the larger bill to the cashier who said, "Wait just a minute."

She ran over to the customer service counter and returned with a three-dollar coupon, which she used on my purchase.

She smiled. "I wanted to help you out because you helped her out. Thank you very much for doing that."

The cashier had multiplied my gift to the young girl. She had repaid a small kindness with a larger kindness. I was so touched and left the store with a lifted spirit having just been a participant in two loving acts of humanity.

I practice these acts because the Bible is very clear on how we should treat others. I know that because I read the Bible and seek its instructions regularly. This I learned from those who came before me. My family, friends, and I often encourage each other with stories from the Scriptures. It seems there is a story to fit every season of our life and every emotion or situation we encounter.

A woman once sought counsel from me during a time of extreme grief. Her toddler had died after contracting an infection. The mother, understandably, was deeply aggrieved.

"I prayed so hard for God to spare her, and he didn't," she sobbed.

I thought immediately of King David and how he prayed diligently, fasted, and wept while asking God to spare the life of his infant baby. The baby died, anyway, and when David learned the news, he stopped his weeping, got out of his bed, dressed, and went in to sit down at a great feast. Those around him were astonished but David's reply to them was the one I shared with that heartbroken mother.

"He said, 'He cannot return to me but I shall go to be with him.'" The moment I shared it, a light flickered in her eyes and a smile of hope touched her lips. She felt the peace in knowing she'd see her baby again one day.

For us, the Bible and its stories give us the foundation that enable us to battle a life that sometimes seeks to defeat us. And to win those battles.

It is truly the bread of life that sustains us emotionally and spiritually just as cornbread deliciously nourishes us.

Chapter 4

BLESS MY SOUL

The normal trend of Southern womanly diplomacy is to sweetly embed words of criticism in words that seem inconsequential. There are women who are so adept at this art that it will take you days to figure out you've been insulted.

Once I was the entertainment speaker for a luncheon during a large, national convention that was being held in Orlando. On a whim, one of my girlfriends decided she'd go with me. I welcomed the company because it can get lonely on the road. So I called the luncheon organizers to let them know I was bringing a guest.

"But please don't go to any trouble. If there's not an extra seat, she can stand in the back."

The woman in charge of the event was a true-bred Southerner, so she kindly scurried around, rearranged the seating chart, and put my friend at my table. Though unnecessary, it was appreciated. After the event, I sent an email to thank her for all the arrangements and to close out some financial things. Her response said, "Wasn't it wonderful? But I am thoroughly exhausted. Never again will I agree to host a luncheon for 1,500 women and seat them all. Last minute changes were the hardest with unexpected guests and such, which can cause such a headache. Still, it was an amazing, beautiful event and we owe much of that to you. Thank you so much."

I got the message. The unexpected attendance of my friend had caused her a problem. She cryptically expressed her annoyance in words of praise. I guess it sometimes takes another Southern woman to decipher messages.

My Aunt Bess, though, would never do that. She is a plainspoken woman, a salt-of-the-earth type who has not lost her saltiness. Still, occasionally, she does try to make it sound a little better. Especially if she has a particular fondness for the person she criticizes.

One day, a friend of hers showed up at church with a new perm that had gone haywire. Her beautician — and by the way, that's what she calls her hairdresser because she specializes in shampoo-and-sets — had fried her hair. It was frizzed and splintered.

Aunt Bess settled down for Wednesday night church and eyed her friend from the moment she walked into church. I knew something was coming, but Aunt Bess held her tongue until church ended. As she watched her friend shaking hands with the preacher, she shook her head.

"Look at Eloise's hair." Aunt Bess's voice was sympathetic. "Bless her heart. Do you think she has *any* idea how *bad* she looks?"

Of course, if you know anything about Southern culture, you know this is a trademark phrase for our women. Any well-bred, ill-bred, or half-bred Southern woman knows that those three words are magic. That's because of the flexibility of the phrase. "Bless her heart" can dress up the cattiest remark, express the deepest sympathy, or denote the strongest admiration. I don't know how we managed to create such a blanket expression but it's pretty clever. Don't you agree?

It is with great interest that I have often thought about the way Southerners use the word "bless." I believe it is one of the great Southern words of all time.

This word can be used to comfort, cajole, and even curse. In the gentle past of my people, when there was no television, movie, or radio exposure to harsh cuss words, they simply used a pretty sounding, Biblical word to express aggravation.

"That blesséd mule is drivin' me crazy," a farmer might say, putting an emphasis on the last syllable and making it sound different from its original meaning. That was certainly not meant as a compliment to the mule.

My ancestors even took the word and added a couple of words with it to express delight or astonishment: "Bless my stars!" and "Bless my soul!" are two of our oft-used phrases.

"Have a blessed day," I often hear folks around the South say, and I've noticed our African-American women, some of the most Godly people I know, have a tendency to reply, "I'm blessed," whenever one is asked how she is doing.

"Showers of Blessings" was one of the favorite old hymns sung by my grandparents in their little country church, though their blessings must simply have felt like a dribble rather than a shower. Quite simply put, we Southern women tend to think in terms of good and favorable occurrences being blessings from the Almighty. The Bible says that "every good and perfect gift comes from above."

"She is such a blessing to everyone," a friend recently said about another friend of ours who is always there with her support, love, comfort, and casseroles in hard times.

We often say the "blessing" over meals, while others might say "grace" or "turn the thanks."

Throughout the history of our people, there has always been a strong tendency to regard our lives in relation to blessings rather than troubles or hardships. In his prayers, Daddy often thanked God for the trials and tribulations we faced, knowing that we would eventually see blessings from those hard times and knowing, too, that difficulties draw us closer to our heavenly Father.

Teenagers probably have more emotional disasters than anyone — or so we think at that age because everything is the biggest deal from hair that won't curl to a broken fingernail to a boy who won't call. Everything is major to a teenager. Unfortunately, or so I thought at the time, my mama would not allow me to wallow for a moment in self-pity.

"I lost the class presidency by one vote!" I moaned, certain that my life was nigh to being over.

"Well, it coulda been worse. You could have lost by a lot."

With Mama, it was always, "It could be worse." She always reminded me too, "Look at how blessed you are in so many ways. I don't know anyone more blessed than you. You can't get down on one little thing that goes wrong."

She was right. We should always focus on our blessings and not on the misfortunes. Mama never forgot one life-changing moment when she had stood on the edge of despair but God heard and answered her prayers and turned her despair into a powerful testimony.

My sister, Louise, was only two years old when a terrible fever overtook her. The doctor couldn't determine what was wrong, but he knew one thing: based on her plummeting vital signs, she was not going to live. There was nothing further that could be done at the hospital so he sent her home for her final hours.

Heartbroken and preparing for the worse, my parents took their adorable blonde-haired baby home. For the next several hours, family and close friends gathered at my parents' home to help them through when the final hour came. And as the Godly people they were, they all prayed. Especially the little girl's mother. As Mama knelt to pray through her tears, she heard the Spirit of the Lord speak clearly to her, "Pick her up, wrap her in a blanket, take her out on the porch, and pray with her in your arms."

Immediately, Mama arose from her knees, went to the bedroom, and did exactly as she was instructed. It was early fall with a little nip in the air, so as she headed toward the porch, several tried to stop her. "Don't take her outside. It'll kill her." Mama paid no never mind and did just as the Lord had instructed. She sat down in a rocker, hugged her baby close, and prayed.

Within twenty minutes, Mama realized the blanket was wet. The fever had broken! The toddler stirred in her arms and became more alert. She not only lasted through the night but by morning she was completely recovered. When the doctor stopped by the next morning to check on her (doctors still made house calls in those days), he was stunned to find the baby in her high chair, eating breakfast and laughing merrily. Not a trace of the previous day's illness hung on her. He shook his head and in amazement said, "This is the work of the Lord. No one else or nothing else could have saved her."

Mama had obediently answered the voice of the Lord, going against practical reasoning, and God had responded by showing mercy and favor. That episode would draw my parents, especially my preacher daddy, closer to the Lord and make them more determined to follow his calling. Blessings, we believe, come from the favor of the Good Lord, and favor comes from living in accordance to his Word, including prayer. When I was young, I believed in luck, but as I grew older, wiser, and more grounded in God Almighty, I came to know that when we walk with the Lord, there is no such thing as luck. The good things that happen in our lives are blessings, and those good things are divinely created. One special story of one particular faith-centered Southern woman is resounding proof of that.

My niece, Nicole, is extraordinarily beautiful both inside and out. She has an incredible heart for the Lord, and like the women before us, she seeks him and his will daily. Faith is always made stronger when it is immersed in the firestorms of life, like gold or silver refined by fire. I actually thought that was pretty clever of me to come up with that comparison, but then, by accident, I came across that same analogy in Zechariah 13:9. The good Lord, of course, had already made that point: "And I will bring the third part through the fire, and will refine them as silver is refined, and will try them as gold is tried: they shall call on my name, and I will hear them: I will say, It is my people: and they shall say, The LORD is my God."

There came a disturbing day when Nicole was being severely tried, and she, as usual, called upon the name of the Lord and he responded. For a few weeks, Nicole had had a motherly premonition that her two-year-old, Nix, was in mortal danger. She had prayed, fretted, and tried to keep an extra watchful eye over him.

Then came the accident. On that day Nix was in the pool strapped into his floatation device. His dad, Jay, climbed out of the pool and turned his back for a minute or two to dry off. In this brief amount of time, Nix flipped face forward in the floatation tube and could not turn himself upright. Another child noticed and called to Jay, who rushed into the pool and found the baby unconscious. Nicole, a licensed physical therapist, was summoned and emergency help called. They worked frantically on Nix, but the situation was dire. On the way to the hospital in the ambulance, Nicole held her dying child close to her chest and she prayed.

The prayer she sent to the Lord was one that only a remarkable woman of unyielding faith could have sent up. To be honest, I don't believe I could have been one of those women.

"That prayer will be forever implanted in my memory," Nicole says. In her testimony that came in the days that followed, she repeated the words she whispered to God in that ambulance.

"Lord, I know that you gave Nix to us and that he is yours. Somewhere in the last two years, I have taken him as my own, but I am now giving him back to you. It scares me to death to think what that might mean, but Lord I'd rather you be in control than me any day. Lord, if you decide to take Nix from us, please give me the strength to face the days ahead. However, if you leave Nix with us, we will give you the glory and honor and praise, and we will spend the rest of his life teaching him to be a servant of Christ."

This humble mother's prayer brings tears to my eyes every time I think about it. Nicole had done exactly what Abraham had done when he obediently offered his beloved son, Isaac, as a sacrifice to God. And the Lord did for Nicole exactly what he did for Abraham—he returned her son to her. Nix lived. Miraculously, the doctors said. When it became clear that his vital signs were good, an emergency-room nurse told Nicole how lucky she was.

"We're not lucky," Nicole responded immediately. "We're blessed. Only by the grace of God is my baby alive."

From that moment forward Nicole has believed that her willingness to put aside her selfishness and give her baby back to the Lord was what gave her baby back to her. It was counterintuitive but she followed her faith, and the Lord responded to that call. In the book of James, we are told that "faith without works is dead." We must demonstrate our faith by actively putting forth an effort to give the Lord an opportunity to work.

> *Was not Abraham our father justified by works, when he had offered Isaac his son upon the altar? Seest thou how faith wrought with his works, and by works was faith made perfect? . . . You see then how that by works a man is justified, and not by faith only. . . . For as the body without the spirit is dead, so faith without works is dead also. (James 2:21 – 22, 24, 26)*

In the early days that followed the accident, well-meaning friends and family would often say compassionately to Nicole, "We're so sorry that you had to go through such an ordeal."

Nicole would inevitably smile and say, "Please don't be because we are not sorry we had to go through it."

Wide-eyed shock would greet that remark; then she would smile again and continue, "Don't misunderstand me. I would never wish to go through the accident again, even if I knew that Nix would be okay. But because we went through the accident, God was able to reveal himself in a way that he would not have been able to do otherwise. I feel like we were able to see the hem of his garment, and for that I am forever grateful."

God had walked with Nicole and her family, and he had sustained them. Incredibly, she had responded to the moment of crisis as only a Bible-reading, daily-praying, constantly God-seeking woman can do. She asked for the Lord's will to be done, not hers. He responded with an outpouring of riches that blessed not only her heart but blessed, most importantly, her soul.

It is wonderful that we Southern women can bless hearts like we do, but it pales in comparison to how the good Lord can bless souls.

Not only do we often benefit from our trials because our faith grows as we depend on it more, others are often blessed by our example and how we deal with tribulations. That's the best kind of "bless your heart" that any Southern woman can do.

Chapter 5

ON A WING
AND A PRAYER

I have seen several godly women pray their men through the gates of heaven. No one can outpray a Southern woman who is deeply entrenched in her faith. Some of my people, mostly those from time past, have been nonrepenting sinners while the others of us were merely sinners saved by grace. It has even been highly suspected, talk being what it is in all places including the South, that a couple of those blatant sinners who adamantly refused to be washed in the blood of the Lamb might have been right-hand men for Satan.

Perhaps, also, you'd be interested to know that those who repeatedly refused to bend the knee and bow were mostly men. But down to the man, they were all married to faith-filled women who prayed mightily for their souls—women who gathered regularly in church to beseech the Lord to save those men who, at best, stayed back at home or, at worse, were out and about and up to no good. These saintly women never gave up on the men they loved. One dear woman found herself not only with one unredeemed husband but also with three sons in a similar predicament. While she was a stalwart member of the church, never missing a service from her seat in the fourth-row pew, her men never darkened the door of the church. For years, she prayed hard and long for each one. It took about thirty years of diligent praying but one by one, they all sought salvation and turned out to be right regular members of the little Baptist church across the way.

Then, their faithful prayer warrior got worried.

"I've been prayin' for over thirty years to see all my men saved and in church," she explained. "I begged the Lord not to let me die until I knew their souls were safe. Well, now that I know they are saved I'm a-wonderin' if the good Lord is gittin' ready to call me home."

That was years ago and she's still alive, kicking and praying. It looks like the good Lord wanted her to enjoy the fruits of her labor, and enjoy them she certainly has.

"The Lord has answered a lot of prayers for me over the years, but none I've 'preciated more than bringin' my boys back into the fold." And then like most Southern women, she concluded with a Scripture that summed it up best: "After all, if a man gains the world and loses his soul, what has he profited?"

By the way, if you ever want to win a battle against a Southern woman, know thy Bible. Throwing Scripture at a Southern woman is akin to throwing kryptonite at Superman. She melts to a puddle of nonresistance. If the Lord said it and you can prove it, she won't argue against it. Unless, of course, she's smarter and can shoot down your Scripture with a stronger one of her own. That's always a strong possibility.

When Mama died, I knew I had lost a lot. Her wisdom and common-sense advice had seen me through many situations while her green thumb had saved numerous plants for me, and her brilliance at getting out any stain had salvaged many items of clothing. In the days that followed her death, I thought of much I would miss: the sound of her voice, her affinity for unique mountain words that are slowly slipping out of our lexicon, her incredible homemade creamed tomato soup, her sewing skills, her words of encouragement at just the right time, and her available-at-any-time babysitting services for my dachshund, Dixie Dew. But nothing would I miss as much as her prayers that had seen me through many quandaries and heartbreaks.

Repeatedly, I thought back to an afternoon a week before her death. I was stranded in the airport, trying to make it to Fayetteville, Arkansas, for a speaking engagement the next day. Flight after flight was cancelled for various reasons until soon I was down to only one flight left that would get me there in time. The flight was oversold with fifteen people waiting for seats to open up, and I was way down the list. Not only did the event represent good revenue for me, but the luncheon organizers had spent a year planning for the event, so I was sick at the thought of letting them down. I had cajoled, pleaded, and charmed but had no assurance of a seat on that last plane.

I struck up a conversation with an executive who had watched for hours as I tried to get to Arkansas. Finally, I took out my cell phone, flipped it open, and said to him, "I've tried everything else; there's only one thing left to do."

He smiled when he heard me say, "Mama, I need you to pray me onto a plane to Arkansas." I explained my dire situation.

"Okay," she replied. "I'll go pray right now. Don't worry. God will take care of you."

Three hours later, the Lord answered Mama's prayers when the gate agent called my name and gave me the only vacant seat on the plane. Fourteen other folks looked mournful as I boarded, giddy with joy and relief. I grabbed my cell phone and started dialing Mama but the phone rang and rang.

(This is a funny story about Mama: a phone company representative had called one day and convinced her to add the service of call waiting. Mama did, but despite my best efforts, I could never teach her how to use it. She knew enough though to know when the phone beeped that she had another call coming in. She'd tell whoever she was talking to, "I gotta go. Somebody's tryin' to call me." Then she'd promptly hang up and wait for that somebody to call back. It was hilarious.)

That night, she didn't answer but when the plane landed in Arkansas, I called her the moment we hit the ground. "Are you there?" she asked as soon as she picked up the phone.

"Yes! Thank you so much! Your prayers worked."

"I knowed they would," she responded calmly.

"Why didn't you answer when I called you earlier?"

"Oh, well, I was talkin' to a friend, and I didn't want to hang up. But I knew it was you, calling to tell me you got on the plane so I wasn't worried. The moment you called and asked me to pray, I walked right into my bedroom, got down on my knees at the bed and prayed. When I got up from praying, I knowed the Lord was goin' to take care of it. I just felt it in my heart."

A mama who prayed on her knees for her daughter, what a comforting thought. What more could any daughter ever ask for?

For the life of me, I can't count or even recall all the times that my friend Stevie or I have called the other to say, "I need you to pray." Strong friendships, grounded in common faith, always seem to dispense with courtesies such as, "May I ask a favor? Will you pray for me?" No, instead, we skip such formalities and dive straight in, knowing that an eager prayer partner awaits. Many times we've prayed together—and even more we've prayed separately for each other. In all fairness to the good Lord, I must say that while he did not answer all our prayers as we requested, he graciously and abundantly answered many and blessed our lives accordingly.

There is one prayer he sweetly answered, against all odds, that I shall never forget. Nor shall Stevie. Nor shall her husband. Nor shall history or the legion of NASCAR fans around the world. I have always counted it a privilege to have been part of that time when God turned a dreary, cold, overcast February day in Daytona Beach into one full of unbridled joy and unmatched happiness, fully revealing his power and his favor.

Stevie's husband, Darrell Waltrip, was, by that day in 1989, already one of the most famous and successful drivers in the history of NASCAR racing. One important trophy was missing from his shelf, however—the one that goes with winning the Daytona 500. It was a dream that had escaped him, though he had chased it all of his life. On the day of the race, Stevie was in her usual spot on top of the five-foot-high toolbox, scoring for Darrell—that is to say she was keeping account of his fuel mileage—and I was seated beside her since I was working for Darrell's sponsor as a publicist. About fifty laps before the race ended, Darrell was running in a pack behind Kenny Schrader, who had dominated the race and had qualified a mile and a half faster than Darrell, who had started second. Darrell's crew chief came over and asked Stevie, as long as the field stayed under green without a caution flag for a pit stop, if Darrell could mathematically beat the field on gas mileage.

Stevie, precise and careful always, took up her little calculator and ran the numbers. She frowned then ran the numbers again. She shrugged. "It means going seven laps further than the rest of the field on a tank of gas." The crew chief looked at her silently for a moment then asked her opinion.

Then, my good friend, Stevie Waltrip, who will pray for two weeks before she tells me that I have a run in my hose, nonchalantly shrugged and smiled capriciously. "Aw, go for it."

I nearly fell off the toolbox. Stevie is the most cautious, most careful person I know. She is not a risk taker. But something in her that day led her to take an out-of-the-box risk. The field, in fact, stayed green. Schrader, running on the same kind of fuel calculation as Darrell, dipped down into the pits with nine laps to go, bringing all the leaders in with him to get gas. Darrell, though, stayed out. The race was live on CBS and they too were doing their own calculating and knew that Darrell was taking an unbelievable risk. With seven laps to go, the camera crew came to our pits to film, hoping, I am sure, to capture our crestfallen reactions for the television audience when Darrell ran out of gas.

But that day, the Waltrips—people of steadfast faith in Jesus Christ—had a crew chief in the sky whose specialty is winning when the odds are against it. As the cameras zoomed in on us, Stevie, nervous and tearful, clutched my hand tightly. "Pray!" she urged me urgently—and we did. We prayed together quickly and then separately. Though Darrell was anxious and kept radioing in that he was out of gas, he stayed out. We all prayed, knowing that his childhood dream was within reach of his grasp but that, scientifically, it was slipping away. God, though, works when science and man says all is impossible.

Our prayers were answered. Darrell won the race on fumes, and then Stevie, true to her faith, tearfully thanked the good Lord on national television for his benevolence that day. When I got home, my brother-in-law, Rodney, always a bit of a wisecracker, couldn't resist commenting on the prayer vigil he had seen.

"I saw you and Stevie praying on national television, and I just have one question." He grinned broadly. "Do you really think that God *cares* who wins the Daytona 500?"

We believed he did, so we had prayed. And as Stevie has said since, "At least on that day, God was a Darrell Waltrip fan."

He cares about anything that is important to us. Big or small. Any need or desire you have, you can always take it to him in prayer. Never hesitate to ask for his loving help.

> *Are not five sparrows sold for two farthings, and not one of them is forgotten before God? But even the very hairs of your head are all numbered. Fear not therefore; ye are of more value than many sparrows. (Luke 12:6–7)*

Chapter 6

GOD HELPS THEM THAT
HELPS THEMSELVES

*I*t's a favorite saying of Southerners, who have always been a bit too independent (that's what landed us in the Civil War in the first place) — "God helps them that helps themselves."

It's also an important component to the success of our prayers and faith — we pray, we believe, and we work toward making it happen. There is an old joke we often share among ourselves about the farmer who was able to buy from the bank an old farm that had been foreclosed on.

The farm had been forsaken for a long time when the farmer bought it. It had grown deep in weeds and neglect. The tenacious farmer, though, took it, rolled up his sleeves, and went to work. When the next summer came, he was blessed with a bounty of crops. The banker stopped by to see the miraculous turn it had taken.

"My, my," said the banker. "Isn't it amazing what the Lord can do?"

The farmer scratched his head, then asked. "Do you remember what it looked like last year when the Lord had it all to himself?"

I remember in college having a hard time in a history class. I had never struggled in history before, but I had started college during what should have been my senior year in high school, and this class was one of my hardest. I was over my head.

"Mama, you need to pray for me about this class," I said, worriedly. "I'm afraid I'm going to fail."

She nodded. "I'll pray but remember this: God helps them that helps themselves."

It was Mama's favorite mantra. She repeated it to me over and over as I was growing up.

The message is this: dig in and do everything in your power to make it happen. My parents taught me many things that have stuck with me over the years, but there is probably not one that I remind myself of more often than this one.

I have known people who will always say, "I'm praying about it, and God is going to make it happen." Then, they sit back in their nice, comfy easy chairs and wait on God. They put no effort toward making it happen. They believe it will be divinely delivered. I know one person who does this repeatedly, and I have yet to see God magically deliver the desired results for that person.

I believe firmly that God rewards hard work, consistent effort, and plain old-fashioned ingenuity. Too often I see people who are chasing a dream become easily discouraged by "no" or constructive criticism. I notice that creative people like singers, musicians, artists, and writers are particularly easy to become discouraged by repeated rejection. My philosophy is this: it only takes one yes to wipe out a thousand no's. The odds are that if you keep trying and you don't give up, you'll eventually get a yes. The odds are greatly improved when you combine prayer with elbow grease.

Listen to this carefully: if you are following the calling that God has placed on your life, you will *not* be defeated. Despite whatever trials and set-backs that you encounter, if you keep going, the Lord will see you through to the end.

> *We know that all things work together for good of them that*
> *love the Lord, and who are called according to his purpose."*
> *(Romans 8:28)*

It's the last part of that Scripture that'll get you—"according to his purpose." Again, that is as simple as following the passions that he lays in your heart. Find your calling, then work in tandem with the Lord to bring forth the harvests of what he sends you to sow.

I never cease to be amazed that I make a living by telling stories. It's really a long shot. Chasing the dream of being a writer and storyteller was a pie-in-the-sky idea and certainly nothing sensible like being a nurse or teacher. But it was a profession that called to me, and while many people tried to convince me to be more reasonable, I stuck with it. Yes, I had rejection. No, it didn't deter me.

Incredibly, my first book, when it was still in an outline stage, sold at a four-day auction for more money than I had ever thought I'd see at once in my lifetime. Then, one day while doing television in Charlotte, North Carolina, a wonderful lady saw me and faxed a letter to me at my book signing. She offered to pay me for a speaking engagement at her college.

Until then, I had been telling my stories for free to audiences whenever the opportunity arose. I felt like I had hit pay dirt, kinda like ol' Jed Clampett. Entertaining live audiences with my storytelling eventually grew into a career for me. But here's the thing: I practiced in front of audiences for a long time without compensation before I ever made money at it. God honored my effort by helping me. He saw how hard I was working, so he threw his immense power behind me and opened doors for me.

One December I committed to doing a holiday event for a bank in Chattanooga. A couple of weeks later, I received another opportunity for a luncheon event in Louisville the day after the Chattanooga event. I make it a policy not to turn down events whenever possible, so I started scrambling to see if I could get a flight from Chattanooga to Louisville in order to do both. No luck. There was no way to fly from one place to another. So, I decided to drive. I left Chattanooga at 9:00 p.m., after finishing the bank event, and drove toward a snow-and-ice storm that was hitting Kentucky. About 1:00 a.m. I stopped in Owensboro for the night, then left early the next morning. It was hard and dangerous, but through the grace of God I did it. God responded by helping me because he saw how I worked to help myself.

The luncheon in Louisville was a huge success, with a standing ovation and an abundantly enthusiastic crowd. In the audience was a lovely young woman named Kelley, who then hired me for a big event in Lexington, where others heard me and hired me for several other events. Because I didn't take the easy way out and did what it took to do both events, I benefited astoundingly. People told me I was crazy to drive through the night in bad weather, but it turned out to be a wise decision. I marvel at how good the Lord can be when we put forth a strong effort.

When I decided to start a weekly syndicated newspaper column, in which I write weekly about the South and our people, there were nay-sayers as well as encouragers. Some told me that I couldn't make money at it, but I believed that if I found the right price-point that newspapers could afford, then I could do it. I have faced more rejection in syndicating that column than I have ever faced at anything, but I keep after it. Usually it takes me an average of two years to land a newspaper! But I don't give up. I just keep coming back until the newspaper editor gives me a chance. And it is profitable since the column runs in dozens of newspapers across the Southeast.

God won't chase us down, wrestle us to the ground, and thrust our dreams and desires in our arms. What you need or want in this life—a companion, a job, financial rescue, your dream, losing weight—requires you to take the first steps. Don't be afraid. Even if you make a few missteps, you'll find your footing again and continue on. Though the way may be rocky at times, if you keep on, you'll find that our loving and gracious heavenly Father will meet you on that road and offer a helping hand.

My friend Kim is an enormously successful real estate broker. She's a go-getter from the word go, as we say in the South. Blonde, pretty, smart, tough, tender—she's got it all, but one important thing about Kim is that she can't be outworked. Even when the odds are against her in a real estate deal, she keeps going and often is able to pull it off. One day she was telling me about folks who would call her out of the blue and tell her that God had directed them to her as a realtor.

"I get a warm feeling when someone calls me and then tells me the Lord led them to call me because I *know*, without doubt, that is favor."

Well said.

Bridget, a long-time, dear friend, and I were talking one day about another friend of mine and the constant setbacks he faced.

"I have no doubt that he knows the Lord, but he … he … he just …" I couldn't find the right way to express it.

"He's not living victoriously," Bridget interjected.

"Yes! That's perfect! That's exactly the right way to say it. He's not taking full advantage of his relationship with the Lord and benefiting from that relationship."

"He's not trusting God for all he has promised," Bridget continued. "That's so sad. I watch so many people miss out on an abundance of blessings because they don't trust God for what he will deliver."

Bridget said it perfectly. Giving our hearts to Jesus is one thing and it's the big thing because it will give us life everlasting. But giving our lives to Jesus on this earth will result in unimagined blessings. He wants the best for all his children.

> *Knowing that ye are thereunto called, that ye should inherit*
> *a blessing. (1 Peter 3:9)*

It's so simple. Our gracious heavenly Father wants us to succeed. Every parent wants his child to do well, but would you just hand your child anything and everything she wants without teaching her the value of working for it? What kind of person would that make? Our values and appreciation are built through what it takes to make success come together. But if you saw your child working diligently, wouldn't you want to make the way easier in any way you could? Of course, you would. We simply must put forward our best effort every day and know he will respond to that.

> *Be not deceived; God is not mocked: for whatsoever a man*
> *soweth, that shall he also reap. (Galatians 6:7)*

Mama practiced what she preached. She did everything she could then put the rest in the good Lord's capable hands. She represented her Scotch-Irish heritage very well because she had uncommon ingenuity. She was always rigging up things and patching things together. Even when all hope seemed gone to everyone else, she stood firm in her faith and her own ability. The power of that combination was awesome. One day she was visiting my house and went outside to look at my roses. At the end of the house, in front of the kitchen's bay window, was a small maple tree I had planted with the hopes that it would grow up and shade the breakfast nook. The scrawny young tree was about five or six feet tall, but over the previous months, it had died. A couple of experts had told me that the limbs were brittle with no growth or leaves.

"What happened to your little tree?" she asked.

I shrugged. "I think someone got too close to the roots with weed killer. I've got to cut it down."

She started nosing around, pinching and breaking limbs, and she found one tiny branch a few inches long that wasn't dead. There was still green in it.

"That tree's not dead," she announced. "All the limbs are, but this one tiny limb is alive so it's not dead."

I shook my head. I figured that it just hadn't died, yet death was coming for it soon. Mama came back in my house, found a small ribbon, and went back and tied the limb to the trunk so that it would grow straight up. Miraculously, that wayward, long limb grew eventually into a strong, enormous tree. It is gorgeous in spring, summer, and fall and even in winter with its long, strong, naked branches. Had it not been for Mama, I would have cut it down and never looked back, but she believed in what seemed to be impossible so I went along with her. That tree will always remind me how important it is to never give up, even when the experts say there is no hope.

Mama had found the tiniest bit of life in that tree, so she embraced the hope that it would grow strong and tall. That hope and her faith worked.

Daddy raised cattle, and every so often there was a difficult birth for which the veterinarian had to be called. One night Daddy and the vet delivered a severely crippled calf. Its front legs were bent back to its stomach and wouldn't stretch out and stay, so the calf couldn't stand. As the vet left that night, Mama was standing on the back porch and heard him tell Daddy, "I'll be back tomorrow and put that calf down."

As soon as the veterinarian was in his truck and gone, Mama scurried out to the barn with two twelve-inch rulers that she had pulled out of a desk drawer and a roll of her ever faithful masking tape. Mama loved masking tape. To our great amusement, she used to wrap our Christmas packages with it. She tore off little tiny pieces of the beige, papery tape and dotted them across the edges of the paper. It was hilarious. It became a huge source of entertainment during the Christmas gift exchange, but Mama didn't get the joke. After all, it was tape, and it secured the wrapped edges together — what was funny about that? Anyway, that night, Mama took the rulers and masking tape out to the barn and went to work. She pulled the calf's legs out straight, made splints of the rulers, and taped them to the legs. She stood the calf up gently, steadied it, and eased it over to its mama where it began to suckle the milk.

The next day, the vet returned to do the grim task and found Mama's handiwork. He went out to the house to see her. "That's a fine effort," he began patronizingly, "but you're wasting your time. That calf will never live or walk. You need to let me put it down and out of its misery."

Not surprisingly, Mama stood her ground. "No sir. You leave that calf alone. I think it will walk again. I have faith."

Eventually, that calf's legs straightened and strengthened. She grew to be a healthy, robust cow that stood on its own. Again, Mama had found a tiny bit of life and clung to it, believing the calf could be whole again. God had helped her who had helped herself.

"If you do your part, God'll do his," she often said. "He'll meet you at least halfway every time."

Chapter 7

BE CAREFUL WHAT YOU PRAY
FOR (YOU MIGHT GET IT)

*B*e careful what you pray for, you might get it," is one of the famous admonishments of Southern mothers. I wish I had a dime for every time that Mama said it to me, pointing that slightly crooked forefinger at me and punctuating the warning with a smile and a wink.

One of my high school girlfriends prayed long and hard for Charlie, the cute, football quarterback, to be her husband one day.

From time to time, Julie would say, "Now, don't forget that my number-one prayer request is to be Mrs. Charlie." So we prayed. And God, as he sometimes does, gave her exactly what she wanted. And sometimes in that sometimes, the joke turns out to be on us.

Boy, does she hate that now. He turned out to be a real disappointment. Bless his heart. Charlie is a likeable good ol' boy with a decent heart, but he's not much to brag about when it comes to responsibility. Given the choice between a hard day's work and an easy day of play, the choice is never hard for Charlie.

From time to time, she'll say to me, "If I ever ask you to pray for anything else again, don't. I'm not smart enough to know what I need to have."

Sometimes, we're just not wise enough to know what we should ask for or what we need in our life, but there is One who knows and wants us to trust in him enough to let him map out our lives.

"God knows best," is my Aunt Ozelle's faithful mantra.

"It's all in God's hands," Mama said repeatedly to me over the years as I confided worries to her. "He'll take care of it." Now that Mama's made it to her heavenly reward and I don't have her to share my worries, I just travel back in time and let those everlasting words of hers comfort me when I need them.

"More tears are shed over answered prayers than unanswered ones," said St. Teresa of Avila.

Rather than praying for exactly what we want, we should pray that God's will be done rather than our will. I like to think I've learned this, but I'm not flawless at it. It takes emotional maturity and a trust in the security of our loving heavenly Father to ask him to let situations work out as he sees fit and knows will be best for us. The human side of us, though, makes it hard to let go and place it in his hands, even as capable and loving as they are.

Jesus' prayer in the Garden of Gethsemane before he was captured and delivered for crucifixion on Golgotha's hill tells us everything we need to know about prayer and how we should pray.

He had already warned the disciples that the impending sorrow of death was near when he dropped to his knees in that garden to pray "that if it were possible, the hour might pass from him." Mark recorded this story in the fourteenth chapter of his gospel.

Jesus then said what we who believe know from both experience and what the Scriptures say: "Father, all things are possible with you."

That's a major reason that we all cling to and rely on prayer. We know that God has the power to turn around any and all situations.

Then Jesus, though he was in human form, which meant that his flesh was weak, clung to the strength of his spirit and prayed what we should all pray when we truly desire the best outcome: "Nevertheless let not what I will but what thou wilt."

That's hard to do. Especially when the most immediate result might mean pain and sorrow. But this I know — the end result, though it might mean journeying through extreme tribulation, will always bring divine deliverance. Jesus suffered horrifically and even cried out at the end, "My God, why hast thou forsaken me?" Following his example might give us reason to question God if we do not understand clearly. I even questioned my earthly father from time to time as all children do.

"Why?" I've asked Mama a hundred times in my life.

"Because I said so," she'd reply. Same with God. Why? Because he says so.

Though we sometimes have to journey through agony and devastating times, our good and gracious Lord won't let us down. He will take us through the valleys and onto the top of the mountain where we will then see "why." And you may do what I have done a few times: lift your eyes to heaven and say, "Thank you Lord for doing your will and not mine. Now, I wouldn't go back through it with a free pass, but I wouldn't take a million dollars for the journey and where it has taken me."

You see, our vision is limited to present and past knowledge. God, though, knows the future, so his will is based on past, present, and future considerations. A friend of mine once fell to her knees and begged God to spare the life of her father when a massive stroke had struck him down. As the doctors frantically worked on him, she waited and prayed, "Please God, please. Don't take him home yet. I'm not ready to give him up."

God answered that prayer and spared her dad, but he was nothing more than a vegetable. He knew nothing and required constant care, a situation he was in for a long time. Then came the time when she dropped to her knees daily and begged God to take her daddy home.

"I learned that lesson the hard way," she says now, adding what many of us have come to know in this life: "Death is not always the worse thing that can happen. There are things much worse than death."

My longtime friend Deb, who grew up in the mountains of North Carolina, once found herself between jobs, a situation that is always unnerving, especially when you're a single woman. Quietly, she clung to her faith and prayed daily, waiting for God's answer. Through those months she always said, "God will answer in his own time. He knows the perfect job for me."

But Deb's mama, like most mamas, worried. One day she called Deb and said, "I just don't understand why God isn't answering prayers. I've prayed and I've prayed."

When Deb told me the story, I shared with her one of my favorites from the book of Daniel where the prophet had prayed for help but help seemed to be a long time in coming. Finally the angel arrives and explains that when Daniel first humbled his heart and made his request known that God dispatched his help. However, the angel encountered a combative enemy, so God's messenger fought the evil forces for "one and twenty days" until Michael, one of the chief princes, arrived to help God's angel so that he could make it to Daniel.

Sometimes, it takes prayers a long time to be answered because the cruel adversary, Satan and his folks, are fighting to keep us from having God's answers. Sometimes God is waiting for the best time when he can bring all the pieces of the puzzle together and make it work. Then there are other times when he is going to love us enough to say no to a request he knows is not for our best.

Humbling ourselves is what the good Lord wants most from us when we pray. Over and over in the Bible, the instruction is to make "supplication and pray." *Supplication* simply means "a humble entreaty," which is one thing I have always loved most about the people of the Southern mountains. Though they are prideful in certain ways, such as in the importance of working hard to feed their families and not taking handouts, they do not hesitate to humble themselves in the sight of God.

Patti is both my trusted assistant and beloved friend. We were friends for many years before she came to work with me, so I have known for a long time what a quality person she is and how she loves and completely depends on the Lord. Patti is a role model for me in many ways. She's content with the simple life and loving family that God has given her. It doesn't bother her to drive a car that is several years old or go without a new dress while her three beautiful daughters have new clothes.

Patti and her husband are financially conservative, and that is a very fine thing because they are good stewards of their money, which is what God commands of us. For several years Patti had been praying diligently to be out of debt and free from their mortgage. Now, here's where you have to be careful what you pray for—because you might get it and it might not come in the way you want it to come.

God answered those steady prayers. And he answered in a big way. In fact, Patti and her husband, Barry, wound up with what we all agreed was a big windfall. At least to us. Now, to the Rockefellers and the Trumps, it would be minor. But it was huge to us. Here's how it happened: the power company decided to build major utility lines running smack dab through the center of Patti's house so using the legal right of eminent domain, they demanded the property. Oh my. For about two years, it wasn't a pretty sight as Patti and Barry fought every way possible to keep the one-and-half-story wood-frame house they had lovingly built themselves—*literally* built themselves. They had lived in the basement of Patti's parents' house for two years and hammered and painted until their house was built.

"I know that to most people, my little house is nothing special," Patti said one day while standing in my kitchen, her eyes glistening with tears. "But it's my house. We built it with our own hands, our children were raised there, and all of my memories are in that house." She sniffed. "And my daddy built those cabinets for us!"

One night, Patti lay down in bed and was praying, asking God to help them spare this house. Now, God was already on his way to answering her prayer to be out of debt, and there was Patti, trying to get him to change his method because it didn't suit her.

"Suddenly, the sweetest peace swept over me and I knew that whatever happened, God was going to take care of us." She never worried again, and the Lord worked it all out just fine. They got a handsome lump sum that enabled them to build a new house debt-free.

"All those years I prayed to be out of debt—and God answered!" She says now with a laugh, "He just didn't answer the way I thought he should!"

Be careful what you pray—and how you pray it—because you might get it.

Prayer is not a magic wand. If it were then everyone would want to be a Christian just to get one. Prayer is an effective tool for communicating with God whether we are praising him, seeking comfort, or letting our requests be done.

Philippians 4:6 says, "Be careful for nothing; but in every thing by prayer and supplication with thanksgiving let your requests be made known unto God." Translated, that means to approach God humbly with thanks and then ask for what you need. You can even ask him for what you want. The sheer process of seeking out a quiet place and turning our worries over to him gives us peace. A few years ago, I decided to take literally the Scripture (Matthew 6:6) that says, "When thou prayest, enter into thy closet, and when thou hast shut thy door, pray to thy Father which is in secret; and thy Father which seeth in secret shall reward thee openly."

I often go into my closet, get down on my face, and pray to my heavenly Father. In the quiet of that closet I often hear him say things to my spirit that I feel quite certain I would miss if I were elsewhere. After all, in the closet there is no external noise, no telephone, no television, no radio. It's just me and God.

"By your friends, ye shall be known," Mama said often when I was growing up. She repeatedly stressed the importance of picking friends with similar values and beliefs. What I didn't understand when I was sixteen, I now embrace completely. My close circle of friends are praying women who love the Lord with all their hearts. Our conversations are regularly peppered with references to our precious Lord, and we think nothing of calling each other up and praying over the telephone.

My dear reader, I urge you, if you don't already have a strong female praying partner—find one! It is so important to have another woman of like mind on whom you can call for prayer support. Debbie, Karen, Stevie, and Pinky are my closest friends. I teasingly call them "The Saints." In their love for the Lord and treatment of others, they are close to perfect. I am the sinner who holds them together, for they only know each other through me. Yet when one is deeply troubled and calls for urgent prayer, I will say, "You got it. I'll call all the Saints and ask them to pray too." Without qualm, each is always happy to pray for the other.

Louise, Nicole, Bridget, Kim, Patti, Gregg, among many others, are also close, loving friends and family to me, and I value their prayers. The greatest love that one woman can show another is to pray for her during trials and tribulations.

One day I was having lunch with Pamela, a friend of the purest Southern upbringing in New Orleans, and we were discussing a potentially favorable situation that had come up in my life. Pamela is a tremendous Christian who follows her Lord faithfully.

"Please pray with me about this," I said.

She smiled. "I will. I won't pray that it works out one way or the other. I'll pray that God's will be done." Her smile grew larger. "And I'll also pray that *you* let God's will be done."

Touché.

Southern women have this kind of loving honesty that is undergirded by our faith, so we can help each other, especially when it comes to matters of the Lord and his Scriptures. Plus, it helps to have one who will speak the truth to us and show us in a loving way when we might be doing harm to ourselves.

Karen was lamenting one day about a friend of hers who always seemed to be tripping herself up with her own decisions.

"I just want to tell her so bad how she needs to straighten up and fly right," Karen carried on. "But I don't because I'm afraid of hurting her feelings."

Instantly, I thought of all the times that Karen has called me up and said, "Now, I'm your friend and I love you, but I need to tell you this ..." So when she said that about her other friend, I quickly asked, "So, tell me. How do I get on the program she's on? Because I think I like the program's she on with you a lot better than the one I'm on. You don't care *what* you say to me!"

Karen squealed with laughter. She knew it was true. But then she sobered up. "Well, excuse me. You do the very same thing to me. You tell it like it is. You know you do!"

Yes, we both do. A good Christian friend using love and tact can help another friend by gently suggesting and being honest. There's one thing I know for certain about Karen: She's always got my back. And she knows the same about me.

> Again I say unto you, That if two of you shall agree on earth as touching any thing that they shall ask, it shall be done for them of my Father which is in heaven. (Matthew 18:19)

When I was a college senior, like many young girls, I worried constantly about my weight. I wanted to lose ten pounds. Every night I prayed to lose ten pounds. Well, God answered. Of course, I lost it when I got mono and was miserably sick for two weeks. But he answered and gave me what I asked for.

So, take it from me and Julie—be careful what you pray for. You might get it.

Chapter 8

SPEAKING IT
INTO EXISTENCE

*S*outherners can be superstitious, or perhaps we just cling to old wives' tales, dating back to the days when warts were dispensed with by rubbing them with a raw potato or burying a dishrag in the backyard. Many of those ancient practices have fallen to the wayside, but some still cling stubbornly to the crevices of our beliefs. For the faithful flock, one of our strongest superstitions is in believing that we should be careful what we say out loud.

"I haven't had a cold in two years," a friend said one day.

"Be careful!" another admonished her immediately. "You'll speak it into existence."

One day Karen called me. A top Southern gospel vocalist, she has been my dear friend for most of my life. The moment I answered the phone, I could tell she was down from the sound of her voice.

"What's wrong?" I asked.

She sighed woefully and went into a story about her new album, which had just been released that day. On it was one of the most powerful gospel songs I'd ever heard. I listened to her story and, frankly, I was a bit unsympathetic because I believed she was overreacting.

"Listen, I don't want to hear this," I said. "You have just recorded one of the best songs of your career. It's going to be your second straight number-one record, and I'll tell you another thing—you're going to be nominated for a Grammy too."

Karen, despite her previous successes and many awards, had never been nominated for the music world's highest honor. To be nominated, she'd have to beat out thousands of competitors in gospel, country, and bluegrass to be one of the final six for Best Gospel Performance. It was a lofty aspiration, but Karen and I both believe that our God is capable of the greatest accomplishments.

Her voice lifted noticeably when next she spoke. "Oh, friend, please speak it into existence."

From that moment forward, I spoke often of the upcoming Grammy nomination. Two months after the song went to the number-one position on the charts, she garnered her first Grammy nomination.

"You helped to speak it into existence," she squealed excitedly when she called to tell me.

When you think about it, though, it isn't strange at all. The Bible tells us that faith is the substance of things hoped for and the evidence of things not seen. Faith simply means believing in that which isn't tangible, that which we can't hold in our hands or see with our eyes yet we're convinced that it exists. The deeper you believe, the stronger your faith is, and the more magnetically you pull toward yourself that which you desire. Though I am a writer and adhere to the magic of the written word, I feel that the mind responds more fiercely to the vibrancy of spoken words. It seems that the words I hear spoken embed themselves more deeply in my brain and are more action-oriented than the ones I see on a page or just think to myself.

Death and life are in the power of the tongue. (Proverbs 18:21)

To work in tandem with God Almighty to bring about what you want, it takes more than just hoping, wishing, or even praying. It takes believing to the very core of your existence, and that is greatly enhanced by a combination of writing it down on paper, looking at it regularly, and then speaking of it constantly. Soon it becomes a normal course to travel the path toward that desire. The Scriptures tell us clearly that our destiny—on earth and in heaven—lies in our words. What we speak and, therefore, believe is what becomes of us.

> *O generation of vipers, how can ye, being evil, speak good things? For out of the abundance of the heart the mouth speaketh. A good man out of the good treasure of the heart bringeth forth good things: and an evil man out of the evil treasure bringeth forth evil things. But I say unto you, That every idle word that men shall speak, they shall give account thereof in the day of judgment. (Matthew 12:34–36)*

On this earth we have a certain amount of time to endure before we can step into life everlasting. So why not use that time to speak of good things that we desire and bring forth into our hands that wonderful treasure? I sometimes have conversations with myself—I talk to myself in the mirror, driving down the road, gardening, or making coffee in the morning. Aloud, I say things like, "That's a great idea! I can do that. I can make that happen." I talk out loud about my plan of action, and by doing that, I speak the treasure into existence.

> *For by thy words thou shalt be justified, and by thy words thou shalt be condemned. (Matthew 12:37)*

I am blessed to be surrounded by Godly women of faith — because I use my power of discernment in choosing them. We often talk among ourselves of our dreams and goals. Not only does that give us the chance to encourage and uplift each other, but it gives us further opportunity to speak into existence — with the agreement of other Christians — that which we want. Sometimes I hear women say, "Women can be so catty and do so much to spite other women." In the secular world that can be true, but it is not true of a woman deeply rooted in the instructions of Jesus because that woman realizes that she is duty-bound to speak good things over her sister in Christ. Choose your friends accordingly.

My dear friend Cindy was born and raised in Mississippi. As a young woman she moved to Nashville to work in the country music business. She is streetwise, common-sense smart, savvy, and completely centered in Christ. Her life story is remarkable in many ways. I've seen her take a lot of hard jabs on the chin, but because of the buoyancy of her faith, she may hit the floor for a moment but bounces right back up. You can't keep that gal down.

Cindy's Rolodex reads like a Who's Who of the entire world, and she generously shares those contacts with any of her beloved girlfriends who need a helping hand. In fact, she calls me frequently and asks, "Have your ears been burning? I was talking about you yesterday. I got someone you need to meet because you two need to know each other."

It was Cindy who long ago began to speak into existence the idea that I should write a book like this. It started because she would sometimes call to ask about clarification on a Scripture or to ask my opinion biblically.

One morning she called, and I walked out on my back porch, sat down in the streaming sunlight in my swing, and chatted about the Bible. After about half an hour, she said suddenly and strongly, "Girlfriend, you need to write a book on faith." I shrugged it off but Cindy would not let go of it. In the months to come, often when we spoke or emailed, she slyly brought the subject up and clung to it as tenaciously as my dachshund, Dixie Dew, clings to a pork chop bone. I always tossed off the idea, but in the manner of strong-minded Mississippi women, she refused to ease up on me.

As you can see, she talked until she had spoken it into existence.

For as far back as I can remember, Mama had a dream that she spoke of constantly. When I was a little girl, Mama would stand at the kitchen window, washing dishes and looking out across the small river that ran through our pasture to a spot on the hill. Many times she would say, "I want one of my kids to build a house over there. It's such a perfect place for a house."

She initially sought to manifest that dream through my sister, Louise. Mama would often say, "Now, when you get married, you build you a house over there."

But when Louise married, she moved to her husband's family farm and turned an old farmhouse into a lovely home. So Mama turned to me. For years, all through my college life and the few years that I was married, she urged me to build a house over there.

"Not me! Never." I was adamant. I'd spent my life trying to get away from home, and I certainly wasn't coming back to the land I had fought so hard to leave.

But Mama, first with my sister and then with me, gently stayed her course for forty years.

"Why don't you just give that up?" I asked her one day, about thirty years into her quest.

She smiled slyly. "Because I believe that one day I'm gonna talk it into existence." I just shook my head and walked out of the kitchen. Maybe so, I thought to myself, but not with me.

I had no thoughts or intentions of coming back home. I lived twenty-five minutes away from Mama, which was close enough but not too close to get caught up in the everyday minutia of her life. However, as the subdivision I lived in grew rapidly, becoming noisier and busier every day, I wanted to move back to the country and find the solace that escaped me in that subdivision. So I began to look for a place. I prayed about it. That, as I have already said, can be a dangerous thing because once you invite the Lord in, he often has ideas different than your own. He laid it on my heart—in a way that made me feel gently burdened—that I should buy that plot of land from Mama and move over there. I was against the idea and repeatedly resisted it. But Mama was getting up in years, Daddy was gone, and she really needed someone close by. Finally, I prayed silently to the Lord, "If this is really your will and I'm really suppose to do it, then have Mama mention it to me."

I have learned this in life—if God ordains it, do it or suffer the consequences of going against his will. He had spoken clearly to my heart, and I knew he had a divine plan.

Three weeks passed and Mama and I were driving somewhere, talking about me trying to find a place to build.

"I feel like I need to be close to you," I said.

She was silent.

"What do you think?" I was prodding without saying it.

In a moment she spoke. "It's been in my heart for two or three weeks that I should tell you that you ought to build over behind me."

I whirled around, tears in my eyes. The same amount of time since I had prayed about it. "Why haven't you mentioned it to me?"

She shrugged. "I wanted to, but I didn't want to pressure you." That, of course, would probably mark the first time she had ever felt she shouldn't pressure me into what she felt was the right thing to do. Nonetheless, the moment she said it, I knew what I had to do.

"All right," I said. "Then that's what I'll do."

The day the graders fought the hard, red rocky dirt and built the road into the land where I would build a house, I walked through the freshly graded dirt while Mama stood contently on the bridge and watched. "I've come home," I said gently. It was one of the most soul-satisfying moments of my life.

She stood on the bridge that crosses the little river and nodded the way a mother does who really knows best. She smiled sweetly. "And I'm mighty glad to have you here too."

After the house was built, I lived within spitting distance of Mama for two years. Twice, I saved her life by getting her to the emergency room quickly, I nursed her through the flu, pneumonia, was there within ninety seconds of her learning of my brother's death, and, importantly, our relationship grew closer and more intimate. She became my best friend and running buddy, because whenever possible, she climbed in the car with me and went wherever I was going.

Mama died unexpectedly in the living room of that house. Her death did not cast a shadow over my home, for I knew that God's divine plan had simply been carried out and that she had departed my earthly abode for a much grander home in heaven. In fact, I am comforted to know that the last house in which she set her feet was the home on the hill she had long dreamed of seeing built. What a beautiful gift the precious Lord gave me.

It took Mama forty years, but she eventually did speak into

existence what would become a wonderful existence for me when I found myself plopped back down in the midst of the kudzu, black-berry bushes, and maple trees of my childhood. Like many stubborn Southern women of her kind, Mama turned a deaf ear to adamant protestations and refused to accept no. She forged forward, speaking constantly what was in her heart, and one day, after many long years, she got it.

We believe in the power of the spoken word as much as we believe in The Word. The Scriptures say that "faith comes by hearing and hearing by the Word of God." That means that when we hear it said out loud, our verbal words strengthen our faith. A strong faith then brings about results.

"Speak as though it were," Mama often said. "And so shall it be."

Faith that moves mountains is given a big boost when we say out loud, "God, I know you can make this happen."

Faith, too, is often hindered by logic, reason, and scientific facts. When praying for extraordinary things to happen in your life, don't listen to the world's facts and opinions. Listen only to what the Word of God says. Jesus spoke very clearly about it in Matthew 17:20: "If ye have faith as a grain of mustard seed, ye shall say unto this mountain, Remove hence to yonder place; and it shall remove: and nothing shall be impossible unto you."

See there? Jesus instructed us to "say" it.

Chapter 9

THE DEVIL
BE DANGED

*I*n Montgomery, Alabama, on a quiet little street, sets a sweet-looking little white-framed Victorian-style cottage with a wood-railed and columned porch and an old-fashioned front door, framed by narrow windows. Six gray-painted steps with black iron handrails lead up to the concrete porch on which hangs a swing, a standard for Southern porches. At first glance, it is so charming and lovely that you would think that only joy and happiness had ever resided within its walls. Yet to the right, once you step onto the porch, you will see differently, for there is a little brass plate on the floor that marks the spot where a bomb exploded that night in 1956, in an attempt to kill the father of the household.

I stood inside the house for a long, pondering moment looking into the bedroom, furnished much like it was on that night so long ago. I wondered what their conversation had been after they had safely tucked their baby away in bed. I imagined that Dr. Martin Luther King Jr. had taken his wife, Coretta, into his arms, held her tightly, and soothed her worries. She, after all, had been home alone with their baby when it happened. For over a year, Dr. King had led a black boycott of Montgomery buses. The bomb was a warning that the boycott should end.

Though I have no solid information to support my belief, I am steadfastly certain of this — that night as they sought comfort in each other's arms in that small, simple bed, they also sought comfort from the Lord. They prayed. Dr. King was an old-fashioned Southern Baptist preacher who spoke eloquently in the words of the King James Bible as he preached in the pulpit of the Dexter Avenue Baptist Church in Montgomery. He used that same language and biblical beliefs as he relentlessly delivered his Civil Rights messages for a peaceful coexistence and nonviolent resistance to segregation. A man of such devout faith is always married to a woman who shares that same depth of faith. Now, the opposite is not always true. But God-called, faithful men always yoke themselves to women of like beliefs.

As I wandered from room to room in that house, still filled with furniture from the Kings' days there, as well as some of their personal belongings like records, books, hats, and costume jewelry, my heart ached for Coretta King and how difficult her life must have been. For all blacks it was a difficult time, but to watch the man she loved step into the line of fire day after day must have tried her very soul. Only a strong woman undergirded by the power of Jesus and an Almighty God could have survived what she faced. Like many proud Southern women of enduring faith, she stood her holy ground. She spit in the devil's face, took her husband's hand, and marched tall and strong by his side.

The people of the South still believe in a mighty enemy that we call the devil. In today's world, where many churches seek to teach only what feels good and preach nothing that would cause distress, Satan and hell are often discarded.

"The Devil be danged," we Southern women often say when trials and tribulations come our way. Emboldened by the faith that uplifts us, we will not be bought by the enemy.

But the Bible is clear: "Be sober, be vigilant; because your adversary the devil, as a roaring lion, walketh about, seeking whom he may devour" (1 Peter 5:8). There is the history of Satan's dismissal from heaven and how he was cast to earth (Revelation 12:7–9). Repeatedly, Jesus talks about him in the Bible. In fact, Jesus mentioned the devil in the Scriptures more than anyone else mentioned him. All one has to do is look around and see that in life there are forces of light and good as well as forces of darkness and evil.

My girlfriends and I talk about Satan almost as much as we talk about the Lord. We know that the Lord blesses us and Satan curses us, but we're also wise enough to know—because the Bible tells us so—that God's power is all encompassing and greater by far than that of the Evil One.

Jesus said, "These things I have spoken unto you, that in me ye might have peace. In the world ye shall have tribulation: but be of good cheer; I have overcome the world" (John 16:33).

While God has a divine plan, Satan has an agenda. God's divine plan has many nuances and objectives that we can't be privy to now, but as the old song says, "We'll understand it better bye and bye." But one thing we can be assured of is that his divine plan is to ultimately increase his kingdom while blessing his children. Satan's agenda is simple—interfere with God's divine plan at all costs by causing distraction and destruction. As the Bible tells us, Satan is the author of all confusion. He wants nothing more than to steal from us the great blessings God has in store for us. Sometimes he uses us against ourselves by tempting the flesh or toying with our minds until we make wrong decisions or let the guard of our faith down.

When that mighty adversary is hunting me down, I often think of my friend Stevie and a summer morning many, many years ago when she told me about a particular tribulation she was facing.

"So every morning, I just visualize putting on my armor for the Lord so that the enemy can't attack me," she said. "I close my eyes and envision putting on the breastplate of righteousness, the shield of faith, the helmet of salvation, and taking up the sword of the Spirit. Then I'm ready to go!"

I never read the sixth chapter of Ephesians, where Paul instructs Christian warriors to do just this, without thinking of Stevie and that conversation. When I am on the battlefield and under full attack from the enemy, I do just as Stevie told me. I close my eyes and put on the armor that my heavenly father gave me. As Paul wrote, "For we wrestle not against flesh and blood, but against principalities, against powers, against the rulers of the darkness of this world, against spiritual wickedness in high places" (Ephesians 6:12).

"Satan is after me today," Karen will say when she calls me. And if it is bad enough, we will pray right then for God to bind Satan's power, for the Bible says that what is bound on earth is bound in heaven. God's power is greater and mightier than the devil will ever know. We merely have to call upon the mighty power of our heavenly Father and ask him to join us on the front lines of battle.

> And I will give unto thee the keys of the kingdom of heaven: and whatsoever thou shalt bind on earth shall be bound in heaven: and whatsoever thou shalt loose on earth shall be loosed in heaven. (Matthew 16:19)

My favorite book in the Bible is James. It is only five chapters long, but it is packed with great advice and strong counsel such as: "Resist the devil and he shall flee from you" (4:7).

There are days when I am under such attack with one problem and disappointment after another that I will stop in my tracks and call out to the sneaky coward: "Devil, in the name of the Lord Jesus Christ, I command you to flee. Flee now!"

It seems to be in an instant that he disappears and peaceful calm returns. Make no doubt about it — Satan trembles at the name of Jesus.

"The devil is trying to steal my joy," girlfriends often say. You may have noticed that when you get a big blessing, it is sometimes followed by something else that just busts your bubble. Guess who that is? Satan cannot stand for us to be happy and resting peacefully in the bosom of God's love. He insidiously tries to take that joy away. Though I'm not particularly proud of this story, I'll share because it shows the very human side of my faith. It is a perfect illustration of how God can send a great blessing along to chase Satan away, nipping at his heels.

One afternoon I was working in my office and checked my email. I opened a message. It contained an incredible, unexpected blessing, which meant a significant financial windfall for me. I couldn't believe my eyes. I was thrilled and threw back my head and said, "Thank you, Lord! Thank you, Lord!"

The very next email came from the editor of an extremely tiny newspaper that was running my syndicated column. She wrote to say that due to space constraints, she had been forced to drop my column. My great joy immediately dispersed into thousands of tiny particles and disappeared. I was devastated. So much so that I forgot all the blessings of the first email and immediately got on the phone with the newspaper publisher and tried to save the pittance that I was losing.

My precious Lord sweetly sent me a monetary bonus in one email and the conniving enemy sneaked up behind in the next email and completely overshadowed God's glory with a nasty little trick. I'm not proud of my reaction, but I learned from it. I recognize it now when it happens. Please don't let the devil have a momentary victory in your life like he did in mine that afternoon. Stand up to him and shake off whatever godly good he tries to undo.

One day my friends and I got into a discussion over pastors who refuse to preach of Satan or hell, and I thought back to my mama who often said, "There is a heaven to gain and a hell to shun."

To be perfectly honest, I am as motivated to miss hell as I am to gain heaven.

I have noticed in other regions of the country that folks don't talk about the devil. But they do talk about him in the South. He's a key player in religion as we practice it, and we are well aware of the power he can wield to toss us about.

> *And there was war in heaven ... and the great dragon was cast out, that old serpent, called the devil, and Satan, which deceiveth the whole world: he was cast out into the earth, and his angels were cast out with him. (Revelation 12:7–9)*

While we know who are our enemy is — this is a good thing because with earthly people, we don't always know that — we believe in a power that is greater and can defeat him. In life's battles, we call upon the name of the Almighty God to protect us. Again, from the book of James: "Thou believest that there is one God; thou doest well: the devils also believe, and tremble" (4:19).

My beloved Aunt Ozelle is one of the most godly women you could ever hope to meet. She's Mama's older sister, so she grew up in the same kind of challenging financial circumstances. Like Mama, she too left the mountains to help make a better life for her family in a place where a living could be made more easily. In her young married life, sadly, she lost two babies in two years. As you can imagine, she was devastated. Her voice crackling with both age and wisdom, she recalled that time of immense sorrow so many decades ago.

"When my second baby died, I blamed God," she admitted softly. "I felt he wasn't a just God. But one night I woke up, and it just came to me. I said aloud, 'I don't understand but blessed be the name of the Lord. Praise Him.' My burden lifted, and from that moment forward I was fine."

Satan had come after Aunt Ozelle with a vengeance. She had given up two babies, and he jumped forward to turn her heart into bitterness and away from God. But he did not win. She chose, instead, the Lord, and she praised him in spite of her heartbreaking sorrow. She also used that time and those experiences to build her faith and become a greater warrior for the Lord's work. For over fifty years, she faithfully taught Sunday school every week. My daddy, a preacher and well-read Bible scholar, often called her for advice and interpretation of the Scriptures because few knew the Bible better than she.

One thing of great importance that I've learned is that the devil always hovers nearby when the sky is raining blessings — or about to. I often say to my girlfriends, "God must have great plans for this project. The devil is firing torpedoes left and right."

This book is an illustration of that. I had previously written secular books, but a smart editor wanted to know more about the faith of Southern women, and my wonderful agent, Jenny, who knows how real my love for the Lord is, enthusiastically brought the idea to me. I loved the idea so much that the moment I heard it, I started shivering with excitement. As Jenny said, "I think this is the book you were born to write."

I believed that too. Apparently, Satan did too because from the moment I set about writing this book, he attacked me regularly. He did everything he could to turn my focus away from the Lord's work by distracting me with earthly problems. Sometimes it was little things like a sick cat that had an emergency trip to the vet or an expensive candle that melted down to nothing, causing a small fire and a huge mess in my kitchen. Sometimes it was things like an urgent phone call that interrupted my writing or a business problem that had to be handled immediately or a laptop that up and quit unexpectedly.

Sometimes it was big things like my mama and brother dying unexpectedly within weeks of each other, completely disheveling my world. But by the grace of God, I was not to be deterred. I knew that the apostle Paul had fought worse, and still he stood strong for the Lord. I was determined—Lord willing—to do the same. That's another thing I've learned in life: Don't be arrogant enough to make plans and think that those plans are written in stone. For the Lord may well have other plans. Let me quote my favorite apostle, James, again: "For that ye ought to say, If the Lord will, we shall live, and do this, or that" (4:15). I grew up among people who often said, "Lord willing, I'll be there" or "If nothin' don't happen, I'll see you Sunday." They were not arrogant enough to think that they were in complete control of their plans.

One morning, a day after Satan had plagued me all day as I tried to write, I woke up to the bright sunshine streaming through the window. I hopped out of bed and literally laughed at my adversary: "Satan, you have picked the wrong person to pick on. You will not have this victory, for it belongs to my Lord and Savior." I cast him out of my day by commanding that he flee. Then I went downstairs to write. It was an extremely productive day. God is always stronger than the devil.

That's how this book got written. I just crossed my arms, stood my ground, looked the enemy in the eye, and said, "Devil, be danged."

And so he was.

Chapter 10

SOFTLY AND TENDERLY, JESUS IS CALLING

The art of survival was second nature to my ancestors. Thriving, however, came harder to them. Still, the Lord wants the best for his people, which is why he led the Israelites out of Egypt and into Canaan. Of course, they didn't obey God's will, so what should have been an eleven-day journey took forty years to complete. The same thing happens to us in today's world: we don't obey the voice of the Lord, which, in turn, leads us to trip over our own stubborn feet and detains us from arriving at our God-ordained destiny. Sadly, some people never finish that journey successfully.

God calls us, but it is up to each of us to respond and to labor to fulfill that calling. A favorite saying of my mama's, and one she used regularly on me when I was growing up, was one that had been passed down from our ancestors: "Idle hands are the devil's workshop." Quite simply it means that if we don't keep ourselves busy doing the good we're put on this earth to do, boredom will lead us into mischief and misadventure. Though those Appalachian settlers had spent two centuries in abject poverty, there came a generation—that of my parents — who had suffered through the bleakest days of the Depression and could take no more. Rarely had their hands ever been idle, because they did backbreaking work to survive those times. But one day, both of my parents separately had an awakening and thought, "Aha! If I'm gonna work this hard, why not do it in a place where that hard work will lead to a better, more prosperous life."

"We knew we couldn't do no worse," Mama said. So she and others of her generation, including my daddy, fled those mountains in droves and went down into the nearest towns to find jobs and start new lives. That would be the foundation for better lives of those offspring who followed, beginning with my generation.

From those mountains they took that long-held creed that had been part of the past generations: The good Lord helps them who help themselves.

With an incredible work ethic, they set about overcoming the odds and building better lives. There are way too many people out there who are drifting through life without true happiness and passion. I often encounter folks who have good, comfortable lives but still aren't happy. And that includes those who are Christians, seeking to live for the Lord. What I have discovered is that these folks are often unhappy because they haven't found their "heart's desire"; they simply haven't followed their calling in life.

"Many are called," the Bible says, and in Romans 8:28 we find the promise, "All things work to the good of those who love the Lord and are the called according to his purpose."

Without a doubt, everyone who accepts Jesus Christ as Savior is called to be of service in this life. Too many people don't know how to find that calling and thus find happiness and fulfillment.

It's simple. Very simple. The passions that lie in our hearts are clearly God's compass to us for the direction he wants us to take with our lives.

Our dear and loving Lord is too gracious to ever call us to do anything that he would not place a passion for in our hearts. He knows that if we love what we do, we'll find success and fulfillment. Some Christians think they should wear sackcloth and ashes and sacrifice joy to be of real service. Not true. Your purpose in this life will be found in the things you genuinely enjoy, whether it's being a mother, an artist, a teacher, a seamstress, a gardener, or a volunteer who helps those who can't help themselves. Or you may be called into the ministry. But listen carefully—God calls many of us to work in the secular world and take our Christian beliefs to an arena of people who might never enter the doors of a church to learn about Christ.

At a women's Christian conference where I keynoted once, a woman, somewhere in her early fifties, came through my signing line. She took my hand tightly and leaned over to whisper, "Please pray for me that I find what God wants me to do in this life."

The face of this woman was filled with peace and happiness. I sensed from her countenance that she wasn't lost on her path in life. She just thought she was.

"What do you do now?" I asked.

"I work in human resources." Without missing a beat, she grinned beatifically and continued, "and I *love* it. I absolutely love it. But if God wants me somewhere else, I want to go there."

"Do you feel burdened that you are in the wrong place?"

She shook her head no.

I smiled and squeezed her hand tighter. "Honey, I've got a feeling that you're exactly where God wants you to be or you wouldn't be so happy. Listen, I can't think of a better place to serve the Lord than working in human resources. You have a great opportunity to touch many lives there that you probably would not be able to reach otherwise."

Southern women are a vivacious lot, who are drawn to fun, and their delight runs joyously through our society. Being happy in who we are and what we do is responsible for the warm charm that identifies our culture and is the core of our Southern hospitality. We're happy, and we want others to be happy in our presence. In short, we believe if we enjoy it and it isn't harmful to ourselves or others, we should do it. It's a simple rule of our existence. That wonderful woman mistakenly thought that she had to suffer in some way to serve the Lord. She didn't realize that the joy she felt came from being in alignment with God's will. The kind of peace and contentment she felt only comes when we are following God's divine plan and desire.

"Neglect not the gift that is in thee" (1 Timothy 4:14) is a strong reminder. We are all gifted in some form or fashion, and the talents we possess were given to us with purpose by the Lord, the purpose being that we are to use those gifts on earth and in doing so, we help others, not just ourselves. I'm a firm believer that if you don't use what the good Lord has given you, he'll take it back. The gift will disappear.

I love what I heard a country preacher say when he stood in a pulpit one Sunday. The Amen Corner of the little church was filled with several visiting preachers. Now, it's customary for pastors of small churches to offer their pulpits to other preachers when they visit. That morning, however, the pastor acknowledged his ministry brethren and noted that he should, perhaps, ask one of them to preach instead. Then he explained why he didn't.

"When God calls you to preach, he 'spects you to do it every once in a while."

Amen, brother. When God calls us to do whatever he calls us to do, he expects us to do it. At least every once in a while.

> *Let every man abide in the same calling wherein he was*
> *called. (1 Corinthians 7:20)*

I'm called to be a writer and a storyteller. It comes easy to me. And it often touches many lives, these words I share through my stories. Not only do I enjoy every minute of it, I make a living from those stories. One cannot be more blessed than that in this life. Our Father in heaven loves us so much that he wants us to be blessed and happy during our short tenure on this earth. When Jesus' earthly parents, Joseph and Mary, found him in the temple teaching the rabbis, he said to them, "I must be about my Father's business."

Jesus' business on this earth was very different than any mission that God has given to anyone else. Still, it is imperative that each of us follows our calling—that is the passion of our hearts—or else we won't be doing what Jesus did: Being about our Father's business.

> *[God] who hath saved us and called us with an holy calling,*
> *not according to our works, but according to his own pur-*
> *pose and grace, which was given us in Christ Jesus before*
> *the world began. (2 Timothy 1:9)*

From what I've seen, there is more personal unhappiness over this than death, divorce, financial concerns, or other earthly worries. If the heart is not happy then the rest of the body will never be. It's the same when a person does not have Christ in her heart; therefore, peace is hard to find. I have noticed that somewhere around the ages of thirty-five to forty-five, those who haven't followed the desires of their hearts become restless, disgruntled, sullen, or sometimes even bitter. Please don't let that happen to you. Follow your dreams and set yourself on the course that the Lord intended for you when you were born.

"How do you know what you're suppose to do?" folks ask me. Again, go back to whatever you're passionate about. What excites you? What do you love to do? What do you look forward to? Think back to your childhood. What was the game of pretend you always played? I believe that our fantasy games as children are really manifestations of what we're born to do in our adult lives. Children are simple and unencumbered by logic or facts. They only know what their hearts tell them to do.

"Suffer the little children to come unto me," Jesus commanded. If adulthood has become too complicated, too unfulfilling, then revert back in your mind to your childhood and figure it out. When I was no more than six, I would pull the family suitcase from the closet and literally pack my clothes in it and then take off on a pretend trip to New York City on book business.

There is only one way that a child from the rural South knows about publishing in New York: the good Lord put that knowledge in my mind when he put that passion in my heart. Books, stories, and words, woven together to create vivid images, were the joy of my soul from a young age. I won reading awards at the library beginning at the age of four. I came home from Sunday school and would assemble the family together to retell the Bible stories I'd heard that day. At nine, I started writing my own stories. The road to living my dream wasn't always easy. It took many years and many setbacks — some of my own doing, just like the children of Israel — to get there, but I knew no better than to follow the passion in my heart, pray, and listen hard for the Lord's voice. No, I didn't always hear it clearly. And yes, sometimes I ignored it when I did hear it clearly. But through trial and error and a loving, merciful God who never gave up on me,

I found the destiny he intended for me. What I practiced as a child, I now practice with my full heart as an adult: I stand in front of audiences and tell stories. I also write them down for people to read.

When she was no more than a toddler, Karen could sing like a bird. To this day, she is blessed with perfect pitch. Her mama would stand her up on a chair and let her sing for family. She began singing in church, later forming a little trio with her sister and a friend, and learned to play the piano. She was consumed with music because it was her calling, and since she managed to keep her heart childlike, she followed her dream of singing Southern gospel music. In college, we both majored in what we love: songs and stories. After college, we roomed together and set about following our God-given passions. Karen was hired by one of the top Southern Gospel groups in the business to sing soprano in their four-part harmony, and I was hired by the local daily newspaper as a sports writer. I went out to sporting events, found stories, gathered them up, and then came back to write them for people to read.

It was fun for both of us, but it sure wasn't profitable. We struggled to the point that we would have to pool our change and count it out to buy a pizza! But we were happy, and so we stayed our course. Over the years, as we struggled to follow the course of our dreams, people who said they knew better encouraged us to give up our dreams. "Get a job with benefits. Insurance. Retirement. One that pays decent and gives you a chance for advancement. A real job that'll take you somewhere rather than nowhere."

There were low points when those folks sure sounded like they might just know more than we did. Here's the thing about a solid dream, though. If you accept it and you nurse it, there comes a point when it wraps itself so tightly around you that it becomes embedded in the marrow of your bones. Then there is no letting go, no matter what obstacles you encounter. Fortunately, Karen and I, both starry-eyed dreamers, had each other, so when one was down, the other encouraged her and vice versa. In those days, we often sat up way into the night, cross-legged on the sofa in our pajamas, and talked of our dreams and ambitions.

And together, many times, we knelt in front of the sofa and prayed for God's guidance and favor.

The week that I signed a new publishing contract and Karen boarded a plane for Los Angeles, where she was honored as a nominee at the Grammy awards, we prayed together again and thanked God for blessing our paths. It was a lovely week, and what was especially wonderful about it was that God allowed it to come together for both of us at the same time, paying tribute to the years we traveled side-by-side, seeking the pot of dreams at the end of the rainbow. We stayed the course through the heavy storms, and we had been rewarded rainbows.

Every woman who ignores her calling, who does nothing to bring her dreams into reality, is a victory for the enemy. Remember: he doesn't want to see us happy and successful. And he especially does not want us to carry out the Lord's plan for our lives. Oh no. He doesn't want that nary a bit. There is something big at stake here, and it's more than just our personal happiness. It's fulfilling the purpose for which the good Lord breathed breath into our bodies and gave us life.

Follow God's calling for your life—and everyone, especially you, wins.

Chapter 11

THE GOODWILL CIRCLE

*A*long-held practice of the rural South is for communities and churches to have Goodwill Circles. These are comprised of caring women who stand ready to help and serve when the need arises. When the loss of a loved one occurs or someone is down in spirit or body, the Goodwill Circle leaps into action. Each member has her culinary responsibility—a casserole to make, a pie to bake, sweet tea to brew—plus another member of the circle to call and pass along the news until it makes the full circle.

When Mama needed sudden, unexpected heart surgery, my sister, Louise, and I listened to the doctor, signed the papers, and retired to the waiting room. Concerned, we held hands and prayed together, but as soon as "amen" was uttered, my sister leaped into action.

"I have to start the prayer chain," Louise said urgently, picking up the phone and calling the first person on the list, who then called another, who called another, and soon the heavens were beseeched with prayers from saintly women calling for God's help on our behalf.

When we suffered a sudden death in our immediate family, the food poured in from all directions. On the night of the visitation at the funeral home, Clarice, one of those saintly, priceless women, came up and hugged me. "Our circle was going to bring food tomorrow, but Louise said there's no need, that y'all got plenty."

"Well, I need to talk to her about that," I replied in a teasing tone. "We don't need to be turning down any food!"

But the truth was that we had an overabundance. Our friends and neighbors had responded to all the times that Mama, Louise, Nicole, and I had carried food to those who were suffering spiritually, emotionally, and physically. The Goodwill Circle had circled back around to us.

> I was an hungered, and ye gave me meat: I was thirsty, and ye gave me drink: I was a stranger, and ye took me in. (Matthew 25:37)

> Inasmuch as ye have done it unto one of the least of these my brethren, you have done it unto me. (Matthew 25:40)

Moments of kindness are important pieces we leave behind us as we travel through life and then, eventually, leave it for the place we'll call home for eternity. These kindnesses are as important to our legacies as the families who represent us when we're gone. Be mindful always of the moments of kindness that will belong to you exclusively and no one else. Each day offers a treasure chest filled with moments of kindness, and from that precious chest, you can pick and choose the ones you will give away.

Cherish them. Hold them tightly. Covet every moment. Do not allow one moment to escape, because once an opportunity for a moment of kindness passes, it's gone forever. It never again comes back around. Once this life on this earth is ended, it will not be the dollars you made that count. It will be the moments of kindness that you leave behind. Strive to leave many behind. This is necessary for two reasons. First, it's a practical practice for all decent people, especially Christians.

In the South, we sort people into two categories: Decent and No Account. Decent folks are often also known as "God-fearing," "church going," or "good Christians." We recommend plumbers and all other contractors based on "He's a good Christian man." Now, of course, that has been known to come back and bite us on more than a few occasions. Still we continue to offer up recommendations for fixing a leaky toilet on such pertinent information.

No Accounts are also known as "sorry," "lazy," "low down," or "good for nothin'." Most No Accounts lay up drunk much of the time, and they wouldn't know work from a rattlesnake even if it jumped up and bit 'em on the hand. Good-for-nothin' people come from "I-knew-even-when-he-was-a-kid-that-he'd-never-amount-to-nothin'" children.

When all's said and done, Decent People tend to breed Decent People, and No Accounts breed No Accounts. It's all in the family tree, you know.

So, most of all, you want to strive to be a Decent People, not a No Account. Acts of kindness are essential to Decent People.

Secondly, what you put out into the world comes back to you. The more good you ladle out, the more good pours back on you and yours. No Accounts have very little good come their way.

> Give, and it shall be given unto you; good measure, pressed down, and shaken together, and running over, shall men give into your bosom. For with the same measure that ye mete withal it shall be measured to you again. (Luke 6:38)

That one's for the Decent Folks.

Here's what the No Accounts can expect:

> *Woe unto the wicked! it shall be ill with him: for the reward*
> *of his hands shall be given him. (Isaiah 3:11)*

I like the Decent People's Scripture better.

Daddy once pastored a small country church called Town Creek Baptist in a place where many of the communities and, therefore, churches are named after the waters that run through their lands: Shoal Creek, White Creek, Blue Creek, Mossy Creek, Duke's Creek, and such. It was one of two churches that he pastored simultaneously since the congregations met on alternating Sundays. I was a tiny girl when Daddy left, but thanks to their many kindnesses over the years, I will never forget the people of that church.

For thirty years after Daddy left the church, Betty and her husband faithfully brought fresh vegetables from their summer gardens to my parents. After Daddy died, they continued to share their bounty with Mama for another ten years. One summer morning, I stopped by to see Mama and was forced to step over several half bushel baskets laden with vegetables.

"Where'd you get all that stuff?" I asked as the screen door softly banged closed behind me.

Mama grinned proudly. "The Dockerys." She shook her head in amazement. "They never forget me. Did you see that Betty even shucked that corn for me?"

When Mama died, I hugged Betty tightly and thanked her for the forty years of goodwill that she had given my mama and daddy. "I shall never forget your years of many kindnesses."

Tears rolled down her cheeks. "We's glad to do it. Wouldn't nothin' a'tall."

Through my own tears, I smiled mischievously. "Now that Mama's gone, do I get her vegetables?"

Betty threw back her head and laughed gaily. "No!"

Well, I guess you can only take it so far.

A ways back in that receiving line were several female members of the Nix family. Miss Ruby and her daughters, also from Town Creek Church, had welcomed us into their homes for large, home-cooked meals many times over the years since Daddy had left the church. Miss Ruby too was always quick to offer hydrangea plantings and other flowers from her gorgeous garden.

"Get whatever you want," she said often. "Help yourself."

Compassion is the sweetest gift we can give one to another. Unfortunately, few people are born with the gift of natural, deep compassion. Most of us have to learn it through suffering, for once you've known deep anguish, you can feel for others who walk those same tearful paths. Divorce, death, downsizing, and other tribulations have whipped my heart into a mush of compassion. Whenever I hear of layoffs, I immediately pray for those affected, for I know personally the worrisome burden of being out of work. I love animals. Before Dixie Dew, I had another dachshund, Highway, who was the light of my life. When she died suddenly, my heart was completely broken. I was so pitiful that many loved ones gathered around me.

I shall never forget my sister, Louise, who came straight to my house to hold me while I cried. And my friends Debbie and Pinky who came too and tried to comfort me. Debbie went out and bought a little rattan hamper to bury Highway in, and my brother-in-law Rodney build a little pinewood box to use as a "vault" for the hamper. On that bitterly cold December afternoon, all of them, plus Mama, my nephew Rod, niece Nicole, and her baby, came to help me bury Highway on the banks of the river behind Mama's house. We prayed, sang "Amazing Grace," and those people loved me as hard as they could. That day, I wrote out a Scripture and placed it in Highway's casket: "Sorrow is better than laughter: for by the sadness of the countenance the heart is made better" (Ecclesiastes 7:3).

For me, no Scripture rings any truer. The sorrows I have faced have, indeed, made me a better person, more aware of what others feel when sorrow crosses their paths.

My friend Stevie and I were talking one day about how teary-eyed we get when we are touched by the trials that others face.

"I just can't help myself," I said. "I feel others' hurt so much."

Stevie nodded. "I know. And I know that others don't understand that. When I get emotional like that, my children roll their eyes, like 'Here she goes again.'"

"That's because they've yet to know deep sorrow in their lives. One day they'll understand," I replied.

It saddens me to think of the lessons these children will have to learn as they travel through life, lessons that will teach them the kind of compassion that their mother and I now feel. Some people, though, never adopt a heart of compassion. Instead, they become bitter and hardhearted. Be careful how you react when troubles come your way. Though tenderheartedness can be painful, it is always the best way. In the end it produces the best results, since you'll be drawn to helping others as much as possible. When our family has suffered tribulation, the circle of compassion has remained unbroken. Loving people have held us in their arms as we cried, cooked for us, cared for us, and prayed for us. Those moments are healing, soothing, and worth all the tears we've shed over other people's troubles. It's an emotional investment that always pays dividends.

Chapter 12

CARRY ME BACK,
LORD

e opened the door and stepped into the backstage area of the Grand Ole Opry. Around us, gospel music stars, some of them legends, bustled in excitement, chatting merrily and hugging each other. In less than an hour, the cameras would start rolling for another in the long series of Bill Gaither videos, featuring some of gospel music's greatest talents.

It was a closed taping session, but my good friend Judi, who handles publicity for the Gaithers' events, had invited me and two friends to sit in and watch. I settled down on the second row between Reita and Linda Davis, a Grammy-award-winning country-music artist. From the stage, where she was ready to perform, my closest friend, Karen Peck, smiled and waved, just as the music kicked off. We all shivered with excitement. Linda reached over and squeezed my hand.

That day at the Grand Ole Opry took us back to a simpler time, a time that we, in our youthful ignorance, were eager to escape, but now, in our wiser, older years, are equally eager to relive. We clapped our hands, bounced our heads along with the melodies, and cried our sentimental tears — so touched were we by the music we heard. Then Karen, pretty and gifted, stepped forward to belt out "I'll Be Satisfied" and wrapped it up with "Old Time Religion." By the end of the taping, I knew why the Gaither videos have sold well over 20 million copies — folks like me are homesick for what used to be. A one-hour Gaither video can take us back to a place when everyone we loved was still alive, and sorrows or worries had yet to find us. It is a sweet place to visit, a respite from our troubles and daily aggravations.

"Thank you so much for asking me," Linda said with a big smile. After a couple of the old-timey gospel favorites that we grew up singing, she leaned over and asked, "Don't you feel like we're right back in the little churches where we grew up? With the old upright piano in the corner that had the keys that always stuck?"

I laughed and nodded. Yes, I could just picture that time long ago when the choir was spontaneous and unrehearsed and the piano player pounded the keys hard because a gentle touch produced so little sound on the ancient instrument. The songbooks then were worn and tattered, and many of the standards were written by the prolific Albert B. Brumley, such as "I'll Fly Away." The song sung during the altar call, when the redeemed urged the unwashed to accept salvation, was always one of the favorites, usually "Just As I Am," "Softly and Tenderly," or "Are You Washed in the Blood?"

It's good to take these trips back to simpler times. For me, it keeps me grounded and makes me reflect on the things I've learned — or should have learned. In the South, I believe, we do a good job of keeping traditions alive, even though they are considered old-fashioned by some. They may think such traditions are antiquated and unnecessary, but they are part of the charm of the South and its people.

We Southern women enjoy congregating, conversing, and carrying casseroles to any get-together that we can conjure up. You can't out-casserole a decent Southern woman who has been raised properly. Here's one of my favorite jokes:

A grade school teacher once told her class that the next day would be show-and-tell for their religions. "I want everyone to bring in a symbol of your faith and explain it to the class."

The next day, one young boy went to the front of the class and held up a rug. "I'm Muslim, and this is a praying rug," and he explained how it was used.

The next little girl held up what looked like a piece of jewelry and said, "I'm Catholic, and this is a rosary." She explained its purpose.

Another little boy, when it was his turn, held up a star. "I'm Jewish, and this is the Star of David." He explained its significance.

Then a prissy little girl pranced to the front and held up a dish. "I'm Southern Baptist, and this is a casserole dish." No explanation necessary.

That's us to a T. A family reunion, a covered dish dinner, an all-day-singing-and-dinner-on-the-ground are just more great excuses for a Jell-o salad, broccoli casserole, fried chicken, or coconut cake.

A good many churches in the rural South still baptize in rivers rather than baptismal pools. Some do it out of necessity because they don't have inside pools; others have pools but opt to take this beautiful ritual back outside. Jesus was baptized in the river too, as you recall.

One summer Sunday afternoon, a host of church people gathered on the banks of the Chattahoochee River, a handsome body of sparkling water that cuts a winding swath through the red hills of North Georgia and lazily snakes its way over a hundred miles down through the valleys and past Atlanta. In its wake, it leaves enjoyment for those who tube it, raft it, ski it, boat it, swim it, and fish it, and thanks to the formation of Lake Sidney Lanier, it provides drinking water for millions.

Few American rivers, certainly none that belong exclusively to the South, are more famous than the beautiful Chattahoochee, which once separated the Cherokee Nation from the Creek Nation and later was used as a border between both nations and early settlers. The lyrical, gentle words of poet Sidney Lanier first immortalized the river in a gorgeous rhapsody known as "Song of the Chattahoochee."

That summer Sunday afternoon, however, hearkened back to the Chattahoochee's simpler days, before tourists, developers, and Hollywood discovered it. Shoal Creek Baptist Church, on the heels of a week-long revival, had shown up en masse to baptize the newly converted. Twelve people of varying ages joined hands and slowly followed the preacher and a deacon into the softly rippling waters between a bend, shaded by massive hardwood trees, and a gentle shoal. As is the practice of the Baptists, each convert, one by one, is ceremoniously lowered into the water, which represents a "liquid grave" and signifies that the person's sins have been buried and life has begun anew.

One young boy, surely not much of a sinner to begin with, zealously proclaimed, "I wanna be baptized and have my sins washed away!" Those who gathered sang "Shall We Gather at the River" and "I'll Fly Away," said a prayer, and formed a line to shake the hands of those dripping with the famous water.

Watermelons were cut, fellowship was shared, and barefoot children, without a video game or a high tech toy, played as their ancestors had. They grabbed a rope tied to a high limb of an oak tree, swung out over the deep part of the river, and dropped into the water with a joyous splash while others swam and toddlers waded. Laughter rang through the trees, and merriment echoed among the sweet sounds of the river ebbing its way to a busier, noisier place.

It was the most beautiful song of the Chattahoochee that anyone could ever hope to hear.

Though the South is home to one of the nation's largest cities—Atlanta—and has many bustling, growing cities like Nashville, Jackson, Memphis, Charlotte, Columbia, Birmingham, and Little Rock, the majority of Southern soil is still rural. Trust me. I know this because I travel these Southern roads where a cell signal has never reared its frequency. In less populated areas, life tends to be more laid back and, therefore, more enjoyable. Thank goodness that church isn't the only place we can find God—otherwise we'd see him only a couple of times a week at most. Of course, our heavenly Father can be found any place at any time, but my favorite place to meet him and talk to him quietly is wherever I find the beauty of nature that he created.

From my back porch, I can swing gently and watch the squirrels jump from limb to limb on the large oaks in the backyard. As I listen to the birds chirp chattily to each other, I close my eyes and hear the Lord speak softly to my spirit. Sometimes I wander down to the creek bank, settle down under the beloved maple tree of my youth, where all my dreams were first cast, listen to the water rippling by, and say, "Hello, my Lord"—and start my conversation from there.

Be still and know that I am God. (Psalms 46:10)

I love that Scripture. Sometimes in the franticness of my life, I just have to stop and repeat that Scripture to myself. Here's what I know: when we're racing through life at Daytona 500 speeds, jumping from one thing to another, we can't hear or feel him. We're too distracted by stress and distress. *Be still.* Just as the Scripture says. When we quiet ourselves, we will hear what God has to tell us. That's important, because from him come the wisdom and guidance we need in everyday life. I wake up early every morning and lie in bed for a long while, talking to him in the darkness of the early dawn and asking him to speak back. Sometimes I go into my walk-in closet, where it is quiet and there is no television or phone, and get down on my face to pray.

Daddy always said that you needed your own quiet place to meet the Lord. When I was growing up, my special place was under the crooked maple that hangs precariously over the creek bank. Later, when I lived away from home in a Midwestern town, where I was miserable, I got a letter from my Mama who recalled how often she had seen me sitting under that tree, "talking it all over with God."

In one letter, her heart was troubled and she wrote,

> Maybe I need to go down to the old maple tree by the side of the creek and talk it all over with God. I have said so many prayers about this situation and so far they are unanswered but surely, surely God is still answering prayers and some day we'll see the results but I keep saying "When?" Yes, I do think I'll see if I can meet God there. I know he's somewhere waiting for me. That just might be the answer. Maybe he just wants me to put forth one more step. So come early morning, I'll try it. I'll probably shed a tear thinking of you in the days gone by and say again, "Thank you, God, for being so good to my baby and please God always keep her in the palm of your hand."

Mama had learned her lessons well from her family. She knew she needed a place of solitude where she could speak quietly to the Lord and concentrate on hearing his words. While she was hurting and worried, she wanted to thank God for his past blessings while she asked for comfort and help. She also questioned "Why?" But God isn't offended by that. He simply asks that during those uncertain periods we still stay faithful and trust even if we don't understand why.

Daddy was secretive about his place. We only knew it was somewhere outside and that sometimes he would silently disappear for a while, then return just as quietly. For some reason, it was important to him that we not know where his secret praying place was. Daddy was sick for two years before his death. His illness often made him weak and unsteady, so we had to keep an eye on him. One day, he had slipped out and was gone for so long that Mama and I became worried.

"You'd better go find your daddy," she said.

I went out the back door, letting the screen door bang behind me, and I saw Daddy sitting on a turned down barrel next to the gate that led into the pasture, just behind a little storage building. I approached him, and he looked up with weary, sad eyes.

"I got down here, then I couldn't get back," he said in a pitiful voice that broke my heart. The illness had stolen a great deal of pride from him.

"Let me help you," I said as he stood up and put his weight on my shoulder. I happened to glance around and saw what he hadn't wanted me to see. His praying place. The place he held special and kept so secret from us. Behind the storage building, against the cattle corral, he had placed several cement blocks on top of each other. He would kneel to pray there, placing his elbows on the blocks and clasping his hands together. And there, where he knelt on a regular basis, the grass had been worn away from the weight of his knees. Two bare spots were a powerful reminder that I had sprung from the loins of one of God's most dedicated prayer warriors. A praying parent is a child's greatest gift. I had one who had worn out the ground beneath his knees as he prayed for those he loved. My eyes filled with the tears, for I had seen not only Daddy's secret praying place but also the seriousness of his prayer life. I wrapped my arms around the warrior and helped him limp off the battlefield.

There came a time when trouble clouded my heart like a big black thunderstorm, so I decided to visit Daddy's secret place, bow where his knees had rested, and pray. Stepping back through the years to a special moment in time made me remorseful that I had not appreciated those good old days when all the ones I loved were still alive. Prayer finished, I stood up, dusted myself off, and took a strong, appraising look around, fully seeing the trees and the old tin-roofed barn for what seemed like the first time, absorbing the imagery and fully committing it to memory.

"One day, should I live long enough," I thought to myself, "I will think back to this very time and think of it as the good old days too."

Every day is a day that belongs to the future as "one of the good old days." So make the most of it now and cherish it for what it brings to the present and what it will mean to the future.

Chapter 13

PRAISE
THE LORD

Mama, like many older Southern women, doted on attention. One day, I noticed a friend bragging on how pretty she looked, and Mama absolutely beamed from one ear to another.

I laughed, "A little bragging goes a long way with her."

It goes a long way with the good Lord too. Wouldn't you get tired if you only heard from someone when she wanted something? Yet if someone came to you repeatedly when things were good and showed appreciation, wouldn't you be happy to help when she needed a favor? And wouldn't you give extra favor to someone who could still sing your praises when tribulations and pain walked arm in arm with that person along life's path?

Through personal experience as well as observations of others, I have come to know that the greatest, most genuine praise we will ever offer up to our Almighty God will come through the tears of our sorrow.

My remarkable friend Susan called me up one day and began the conversation by saying, "I just wanted to thank you for all your prayers."

Susan's sixteen-year-old daughter, Shannon, had passed away from an accidental death a week earlier. I was amazed that in her pain, Susan would think to call me so quickly and thank me.

She continued, "The grace of God is so good. I don't know how anyone could make it through something like this without the Lord. I praise the Lord that I will see my child again. If I didn't have that assurance, they'd have to bury me too."

One of my favorite responses in the Bible came from Job, when his wife urged him to "curse God and die" after their lives had been plagued with tragedy and loss. It is safe to say that she did not have the praising spirit of the Southern women I know best.

Job replied, "Thou speakest as one of the foolish women speaketh. What? Shall we receive good at the hand of God and shall we not receive evil?"

As a precious childhood friend of mine lay dying, his previously strong, muscular body ravaged by pancreatic cancer, his testimony for the Lord remained strong and true. I have often thought that Ronnie's Christian witness through dying touched more people than mine ever has through living. He was amazing. One night he told me about someone who had visited him shortly after he returned home from a hospital stay. That person had questioned why God would allow such a horrible, terminal illness to fall upon such a young man and one who had been so faithful in church and spirit for all his years.

"It's so unfair," the visitor commented. "Don't you question why God would let this happen to you?"

Ronnie was firm in his response because he never wavered in his love and belief for the Lord Jesus Christ, even as he edged toward an earthly demise, one he did not want at all. He wanted to live. He prayed to live. But he was willing to graciously and humbly accept God's will. He kept saying, "I want God's will to be done." His eyes would fill with tears. "Whatever that will is." So when someone asked if he ever asked, "Why me?" his response came immediately.

"No," he replied. "I never question it."

"Well, you're a better person than me then."

He smiled. "If I asked him why I have to face this now, then I would have to ask him why he has given me so many blessings in my life. I've never questioned him about my blessings, so I won't question him about my troubles."

"The Bible says that rain falls on the just and the unjust," I said quietly when he told me the story.

"Right. I've had plenty of sunshine, and now I have some rainstorms. But through it all, I still thank God."

Thanking God should be automatic in our lives. There was a time years ago when things were financially challenging for me, as it often is for any young person starting out in life. I was so grateful every month, when I was able to stretch my meager paycheck to pay my bills, that I would whisper, "Thank you, Lord" when I had finished putting the checks in envelopes. These days, things are much more blessed, but still every month when I pay bills, it is automatic to me to still whisper, "Thank you, Lord." Over the years, it simply has become habit.

> I will praise the Lord according to his righteousness: and will
> sing praise to the name of the Lord most high. (Psalms 7:17)

Of course, it's always easier to praise him in the good times than in the hard ones. On the surface, it goes against good common sense to praise him and thank him for the challenging times that come our way, but that kind of praise does the most for us. It will uplift our spirits at a time when we are most downtrodden, and it will show God that we love him no matter what. Our heavenly Father, just like our earthly father, will be warmed by that reaction and respond to it by lifting us up out of the depths of troubles and tribulations. Whenever I think of this, I am reminded of two wonderful Southern women who practiced that in the face of heartbreaking upset.

My sister's best friend, Tammy, is one of the most delightful women you'll ever meet. She personifies Southern female perfection. She is beautiful, charming, smart, compassionate, brimming with personality, and has an incredible work ethic. You can't outsmile her or outwork her. She is also deeply rooted in her faith. She loves the Lord from the top of her Scotch-Irish red head to her always manicured toenails. When Tammy suffered a personal tragedy, our hearts broke to pieces and fell to the ground to join the pieces of her broken heart.

Of Tammy's three children, Amanda was the youngest and the most like her mama in looks and personality. At seventeen, Amanda was a vibrant, lively spirit with a creamy white complexion and thick red hair that exactly matched her mama's. She was a typical cheerleader, always in the center of the fun and leading the troops with a rallying cry for victory. One night, after one of their relatives had died, I ran into Tammy and Amanda at the funeral home. I plopped down on the sofa beside them as both giggled and told delightful stories.

"Well, we better be going," Tammy said finally as she nudged her baby's arm. "We gotta get to the football game before kickoff."

Cheerful good-byes were said, and I smiled as I watched the pair sashay happily out the door, thinking how beautiful both were in spirit and body. Two weeks later, I would see them again at the funeral home, but this time the sad occasion was to mourn Amanda, who had been killed in a car wreck on the way home from cheerleading practice one night. After missing a curve, she had been airlifted to a critical-care hospital, but she died a few hours later. It goes without saying that her mama was devastated beyond words. I shall never forget the moment that Tammy taught me the importance of praising God in the midst of heartbreak.

Amanda's body had been severely damaged, so not only was the casket closed but Tammy had been advised against seeing her baby after she died. So she had not been able to look at Amanda one last time and have closure. By an odd twist of fate, the eleventh-grade class, of which Amanda was a member, received their senior rings, ordered months before, on the day after her fatal accident. School officials took the ring to Tammy, who wanted it placed on Amanda's finger in the casket. Hundreds of people showed up to pay their respects at the visitation that night and I was among them. When I finally made it through the line to Tammy, I took her in my arms and hugged her tightly. She cried woefully and I cried too. Suddenly, her tears stopped. Then, she pulled back, squeezed my hands in hers and with a big smile, she told me of the class ring.

"I didn't have peace because I didn't get to see her after the accident," she explained. "I was standing there when the undertaker opened the top of the casket just enough to slip the ring in and I saw that beautiful, bright red hair of hers." She smiled brighter. "When I saw her hair, peace just swept all over me." She threw back her head with a tearful laugh. "Ain't God good? Oh, he's so good! He knew what I needed and he gave it to me." She hugged me again. "*God is so good*. Praise his name!"

I shall never forget that moment or what Tammy, a true woman of God, taught me that night, even though sorrow clung to her like a rain-soaked cotton dress. If a mama can suffer through the sudden, tragic loss of her daughter and still praise God mightily, then I can surely do it—and must do it—when whatever lesser burdens cast themselves on my life. I have no doubt that the good Lord looked down on Tammy that night as she stood in front of that casket and said, "Well done, my good and faithful servant. Well done."

I will not leave you comfortless: I will come to you. (John 14:18)

I don't believe I've ever seen the death of a parent affect a child more profoundly than when my best friend Karen's father died. He died within two months of being diagnosed with cancer, and although Karen would eventually come to terms with his departure, she would never get over it completely. In tribute to her dad, she wrote and recorded a beautiful song called "Daddy's Home," in which she recalls her childhood happiness when her mama would holler out to the children every day, "Daddy's home!" The final verse deals with his death and his going to heaven to be with the Lord. Karen concludes, "Daddy's home."

Her sorrow was so deep that it was painful to watch during the first couple of days after his death. She was pitiful in her heartbreak, but she is truly one of the most faithful people I have ever been privileged to know. She sought God's comfort during one of the greatest earthly tests she would ever face. The night before the funeral, she sat down and wrote her daddy a tear-stained letter, which, the next morning, she slipped into his coat pocket. In the letter, she shared personal, special memories, thanked him for the great and loving father he had been to her, and she had one special request: "When you see Jesus, please put your arms around him and hug him for me and tell him *I still believe*."

Through the worst personal heartbreak she had ever faced, Karen rose above her agony to reaffirm her love and belief in her Lord and Savior. Those are the kind of moments that distinguish the true in faith from the mild in faith. In the Lord's army, this incredible faith separates the officers from the soldiers because they have earned their promotions by staying the course and adhering to the directions from the Commander-in-Chief.

When death stealthily visited my family, taking three of our loved ones within a period of seventy-five days, I thought my heart could not bear the immense and shocking losses. First, my brother, then my uncle, and finally, the hardest of all, my mama. For two nights, as Mama laid in her coffin, hundreds of people filed through the funeral home to pay their respects and mourn with us. They were heartbroken for us. One preacher commented, "Y'all have been through so much. I'm so sorry to see such suffering at one time in one family."

I took his hands in mine, and as tears flooded like a rushing river down my cheeks, I replied, "But our God is still our God. We love him as much today as we loved him seventy-six days ago. We are broken in heart but not in spirit. He will see us through."

The man, whom I barely knew, grabbed me in his arms and hugged me. When he pulled back, tears spilled from his eyes, and he smiled. "That is the greatest testimony I have ever heard."

Praising the Lord through chimes of laughter and joy is wonderful. After all, whenever we're gifted. we want to say "thank you" to the giver. Praising the Lord through tears of sorrow is a testimony to our belief in and obedience to a divine power. When loved ones have passed on, I have never seen it as a punishment to me. I have always viewed it as a reward to them. They had earned a rest from the labors that have wearied them. Everyone has a place in the lap of the Lord.

I had good training, you see. I learned from all the brave women who went before me, including my mama, who had held her head up bravely over the loss of her only son.

"The Lord has not forsaken me," she said firmly in the weeks after his death. "He will see me through."

Yes, the South has known its share of troubles and tribulations, probably more than any other region of the country. It has also known successes and great triumphs. The same can be said about our women. We have known much trouble and tribulation, but we have also seen much in the way of God's benevolent grace. When times are hard and hearts are hurt, we have to focus on the blessings, for, thanks to his wonderful mercy, there is always light in the blackest of nights. In the dark days that followed those deaths, I sought God at every turn. And always I thanked him for the good he had wrought—Mama had died suddenly and without pain or suffering—and asked God to hold me in his arms until I could hold myself up again. And he did.

Praise the Lord.

Chapter 14

GLORY BE

We had just finished a big Southern brunch on Christmas morning when I coaxed my sweet Aunt Kathleen to the piano.

"Please sing 'Beautiful Star of Bethlehem' for me," I pleaded.

Aunt Kath was a Carder before she married, and though she is not directly descended from the famous Carter Family of Virginia — June Carter was married to Johnny Cash — she has the same Appalachian purity in her voice as those country music pioneers. It is a sound that's hard to duplicate with its haunting and humble sincerity. Like others in her family, she plays the piano by ear. If she hears it, she can play it.

She finished playing my request, then turned to the rest of us gathered round. "Y'all jump up here and help me."

Though I can't sing — tone deaf from too many years around powerful race cars — I joined in, and we harmonized through hymn after hymn.

My sister's mother-in-law sat on the sofa close by and sang every word of every song. At one point, she raised her hand in praise, closed her eyes, and a tear fell as she praised the Lord.

"That's pretty singin'," she commented. "I just want to thank the Lord for saving my soul. Now, sing another one."

Here's what gets me about that story: Mama B has Alzheimer's and has suffered from it for many years. She has forgotten her past, what she had for breakfast minutes before, and she doesn't know her children.

"Now, tell me agin what your name is," she says after a few minutes.

"I'm Rodney. I'm your middle son."

"That so? Well, you're a good looking boy." A few minutes later, she'll ask again.

She has forgotten her entire life. But she has not forgotten her Lord or that she has eternal salvation. She has not forgotten one word of any song that is sung to worship him.

Alzheimer's has robbed her of everything, but it cannot take from her the gift of eternal life. More than anything I've ever seen, that testimony assures me of God's promise — nothing can separate us from his love and grace.

Glory be, as our women often say.

> *Who shall separate us from the love of Christ? Shall tribu-lation, or distress, or persecution, or famine, or nakedness, or peril, or sword? . . .*
>
> *Nor height, nor depth, nor any other creature, shall be able to separate us from the love of God, which is in Christ Jesus our Lord. (Romans 8:35, 39)*

Somehow, somewhere in time, Southerners began substituting the words *glory* and *glory land* for *heaven*. And like the word *bless*, we Southerners, especially our women, picked it up and made a phrase out of it. "Glory be," expresses astonishment, mild surprise, or just plain ol' praise.

"Papa's gone to glory now," one friend often says when she starts a story about her grandfather.

"When I get to glory land, all the sorrows of this ol' vale of tears and sorrow will be behind me," Daddy said repeatedly.

It's such a lovely word substitution, though no one seems to know for sure how it got started. I suspect that generations of Southerners, being the serious Bible readers they were, picked it up because the word *glory* is used hundreds of times in the Scriptures. The Bible refers to "the glory of God," "a crown of glory," "he is the king of glory," "glory, honor and peace," "the riches of his glory," "glory at the appearing of Jesus Christ," and "his glory shall be revealed." For Southerners, no doubt—especially those who struggled to survive hard times—*glory* became synonymous with *heaven*. Frankly, I love it because *glory* sounds so, well, glorious. Happy, magnificent, joyous, fabulous. "In my father's house are many mansions," Jesus said in the book of John. "If it were not so, I would have told you. I go to prepare a place for you."

When the Lord called for Mama, his ever-faithful servant, the preacher who joined us at her deathbed later said that in all his years of ministry, he had never seen such a sweet scene of faith as he saw from our family. Of course, we were heartbroken. But that was our earthy, carnal feelings. We knew she had found the glory she had sought for all her years. Tears dripping down our cheeks, we held hands and sang hymns like "O Come Angel Band" and "Precious Memories," and then I, more tone deaf than not, began to sing a song, more than a hundred years old, that both Mama and I had grown up singing in church. At that moment, I thought its words said it best for Mama:

I've a home prepared where the saints abide,
Just over in the glory land;
And I long to be by my savior's side,
Just over in the glory land.

Just over in the glory land,
I'll join the happy angel band;
Just over in the glory land,
Just over in the glory land,
There with the mighty host I'll stand
Just over in the glory land.

Through my liquid sorrow and woeful pain, I felt the Lord's strong presence in that room. It was if he had reached down and touched me to reassure me that all was just as I had always believed: Glorious heaven awaits all those who are prepared for it. It was a rare moment of incredible sadness mixed with remarkable joy. Yes, Mama was gone. That was the sadness. But Mama had finished her long journey and stepped through the golden gates into the glory land.

"Glory be," I whispered under my breath.

In churches throughout the region, Southerners have always taken great joy in music that worships the Lord, whether formal church hymns, praise choruses, or Southern gospel music. We are a people who rejoice through song. It is integral to the maintenance of our faith. Music is tremendously important to the South as evidenced by the fact that most of America's music has arisen from within our boundaries: jazz, blues, country, bluegrass, hip hop, rock and roll, and Southern gospel.

When I was growing up, it was the fervent wish of every decent God-fearing Southern mama and daddy that their little girls should someday play the piano in church. This, next to finding a good man to marry, was paramount to respectability. After all, no service is greater than that of serving the Lord. So every little girl lined up for weekly piano lessons, some of us taking from accomplished piano players (*pianists* is too fancy a word for the rural South), who taught from their upright pianos, in crowded living rooms, with the doors shut to close off the family activity in the rest of the house.

Some little girls were good at it. Some were not. Like me. Still, it was my daddy's chief wish that my sister, Louise, and I should learn well enough to "be able to sit down at the piano and play any song the choir wants to sing." Louise can do that. I can't even come close.

Another Southern tradition that began in the early 1800s was that of the annual singing schools. For a week or two every year — usually in the summer — traveling singing-school teachers would alight at churches and teach willing participants the art of shape-note singing. In this method, each note is assigned a different shape to indicate pitch on the do-re-me chart. The result was great harmonies that eventually gave rise to our legendary quartet and convention singing. It too resulted in the music taking a place of equal standing in our churches, alongside the preaching and praying.

Over the years, the tradition would evolve into the practice of having an "all-day singing and dinner on the ground." To translate the vernacular of our people, that means we would have a service of singing in the morning, break for a covered dish dinner spread outside on the tables under shade trees, then reconvene in the afternoon for more singing inside the church house.

Those were wonderful times as glory rang out, loud and proud, in the harmonious voices of those who gathered.

Now back to the matter of piano playing by untalented hands. That would be me.

One Sunday a few years ago, Mama and I decided to visit a little country church high in the mountains, tucked between massive rolling hills amidst large oak and maple trees that hover majestically over the sweet white-painted church. Nearby are the sparkling waters of the Chattahoochee River, where the church baptizes their newly converted. I stopped by to pick Mama up, and as she was settling into the car and snapping her seatbelt, I said—because I have no more sense than to open up a can of worms—"I changed clothes three times this morning before I settled on wearing this."

Now, you must know that Mama and I were constantly in debate over my hair and clothes. She often said, "You know, I liked your hair much better back when you used to comb it." A lesser child could never have taken it, but, actually, it rarely annoyed me. I could give as good as she, so it often led to good repartee. That morning, when I stupidly mentioned the black, sleeveless dress I was wearing, which was hemmed just above the knee, she threw a sideward glance toward me and commented. "And then got one that barely covers your tail." She shook her head.

I bit the inside of my lip and said not a word. I had learned not to get in an argument on the way to church. No sense having the devil plop down on the pew and sit between us during the sermon.

We arrived for church just moments before it started and greeted those we hadn't seen in the previous two years, since we'd last attended service at that church.

"Do you play the piano?" asked Tony, one of the deacons.

"I used to," I replied, without thinking how unusual the question was. It had been many years since I touched the keys of a piano.

"Hey!" he called toward the choir loft. "Ronda can play the piano."

My eyes flew wide and my mouth dropped. I spun my head around in shock and, speechless, gawked at him.

"We ain't got no piano player today, and we prayed that the Lord would send us one." He smiled broadly. "And he sent us you."

"Well, he didn't send much. I can tell you that," I replied.

And that's how I came to play the piano for the first time in fifteen or twenty years for a church service. They had to sing what I could play, which wasn't much, but we did find six songs. To say I was awful would be kind. But we managed.

"When you ain't got nothin'," a little lady said after the service, "*anything* will do."

Driving home, Mama and I talked about the experience in a head-shaking, eyebrow-scratching kind of way.

"Daddy used to say, 'Humble yourself before God.' I don't think I've ever been more humbled," I commented.

"What really amazed me," Mama replied in earnest candor, "was how you weren't a bit embarrassed by how bad you were."

Behind my sunglasses, I rolled my eyes. Of course, I knew I was bad but a little moral support at the moment would have been nice. After all, I hadn't touched a piano in a generation. I ignored it and moved on in the conversation, a foolproof tactic during those kinds of conversations.

"You know what I kept thinking while I was playing?" I asked with a light chuckle. "How much daddy must be laughing about it up in heaven. He always wanted me and Louise to be able to play perfect in church."

"You know what I kept thinking?" she asked.

"What?"

"That I couldn't believe that you were sitting on a piano bench in the middle of church in a dress that barely covered your tail."

Glory be.

Chapter 15

YE SHALL REAP
WHAT YE SOW

*M*ama said it often. She reminded me from early childhood that whatever I did—good or bad—would bounce back to me in an undeniable harvest of the same. Doing right, she said, never brought wrong into your life. When I was eighteen and a boy I had dated, who was a bit too adventurous and unruly, wound up in some trouble, Mama smiled knowingly and pointed that crooked forefinger at me with great authority.

"Ye shall reap what ye sow," she announced for the thousandth time. "And he's reaping what he sowed." Of course, I rolled my eyes as teenagers often do, but as the years unfolded, I came to believe in the wisdom of her words as surely as I believe in a sun that rises each morning and rivers that run to the sea.

There again, Mama was going back to the scriptural teachings of her upbringing. I know that the Bible's ancient truths, which had served my parents and grandparents well, are as solid and pertinent today as they were hundreds of years ago.

> *Be not deceived; God is not mocked: for whatever a man*
> *soweth, that shall he also reap. (Galatians 6:7)*

It makes plenty of sense, though, doesn't it? That an investment of good will return dividends of good, and an investment of bad will be multiplied back in the same form. My friend Barbara is married to a famous, almost legendary man, but she is no shrinking violet who has ridden through life on his coattails. She has made significant contributions to society through writing, speaking, and charitable involvements. She is a blazing Christian who stands strong for the Lord and reflects her Savior through the ethical, honest treatment of everyone with whom she comes into contact.

Someone in an organization I had done a speaking engagement for called me one day and asked if I could help get Barbara for another event they were doing. I was happy to help make the connection, so I called Barbara, told her the date, and she agreed. At the same time, someone else from the organization—you gotta love committees—called a speaker's agent to ask him about booking Barbara sometime. Now, an agent who booked her would be entitled to at least a 20-percent commission, but Barbara wouldn't have to pay a commission if she accepted the offer through me. The agent had called her before I did, and he asked about the date. He didn't tell her, however, which organization it was for. When she found out it was the same event, she did not justify it or slip into a gray area. Many people would have taken the way out by going with my fee-free contact. But not Barbara.

"I'm going to pay him his commission," she said firmly. "It's the right thing to do."

The good Lord blesses Barbara and her family over and over because she and her husband conduct themselves this way consistently. You can never go wrong by doing the right thing.

Barbara had long believed that the town in which she lives needed more Christian education. Since she and her family are devout Catholics, she set her mind and heart on establishing a Catholic school. After many years of chasing that dream, it eventually became reality. Then Barbara, even though she was very comfortable in life in all ways, decided that she was going to become a real-estate agent. I thought it was sheer craziness. I stopped by to see her one day, and she was telling me how hard the classes were and that she was struggling.

"I take copious notes, I study diligently, but I still have problems with it all."

I shook my head as I scoured her textbooks and saw all the notes she had scribbled in margins and all the passages she had highlighted. It was evident that she was working hard.

"Let me ask you something," I began. "You have a great life."

She nodded firmly. "I have the *greatest* life." Barbara talks a lot in italics.

"You're blessed financially," I continued.

"I have *more* than I'll *ever need*."

"You get to travel and go wherever you want, whenever you want," I said.

"Yes! God is *so good* to me."

"Then, why would you take on something so hard at an age where you have earned the right to relax and enjoy life with your children and grandchildren?"

Barbara scooted closer to me on the sofa, looked me in the eye, and said with deep conviction, "Because this new school means so much to me that I want to earn every penny I can and give it to the school."

Argument won. Barbara, determined, earned her real-estate

license and then committed every penny she made for the first few years to that school. The Lord blessed her abundantly because she was a good and faithful servant.

"It is amazing how well I've done," she said one day. She shook her head in disbelief. "It's like picking up money!"

I laughed. "You can't outgive God, can you?"

"No ma'am! You sure can't!"

I believe that tithing is one of the most important ways that we sow and reap. In Malachi, we're told that if we don't give tithes—10 percent of our earnings—then we're robbing God. Whoa! That's a scary thought, isn't it? We are also told specifically to render unto Caesar that which is Caesar's and unto God that which is God's. Everything we're blessed with is a gift from God, so giving him back 10 percent of that is like writing a thank-you note, except it's in the form of a check rather than written on beautifully embossed stationery. There again, I go back to my mountain kinfolks who often paid the preacher with vegetables, pigs, and chickens.

> Bring ye all the tithes into the storehouse, that there may be meat in mine house, and prove me now herewith, saith the Lord of hosts, if I will not open you the windows of heaven, and pour you out a blessing, that there shall not be room enough to receive it. (Malachi 3:10)

One Sunday I was visiting my sister's church, and her pastor was making a plea for the Baptist Children's Home. The following Sunday they planned to take a special offering, so he said, "Pray about it. Ask the Lord what you should give."

I take seriously the Bible's instructions to take care of widows and orphans, so I knew that I was going to give. I actually had an amount in mind, which I thought was significant. Apparently, God's idea of significant and mine are quite different because when I prayed about it, he spoke to my spirit and named a number much higher. When he dropped the number into my spirit, it was like he dropped a nine-pound hammer on my head.

"God!" I exclaimed unto the heavens. "You can't be serious!"

He responded by reminding me that the next day I had a speaking engagement that paid exactly what he had told me to give. My shoulders slumped. Though God loves a cheerful giver, I wasn't joyous, but I knew better than to not do what I was commanded to do. I opened the checkbook and glumly but obediently wrote a check for exactly what he said. God probably doesn't expect us to always be happy and eager to do what he says, but he does expect us to be obedient. I'm sure it's safe to say that Abraham wasn't jumping up and down for joy over the prospect of offering his son, Isaac, for a sacrifice either.

But here's what happens when you obey God: he opens the floodgates of heaven and lets blessings pour over you. I gave that check, and within days he had bountifully returned that money to me. Just like he promises he will do if we do as he directs. The money came back in interesting ways, starting with the speaking engagement the next day. The lady handed me the check in an envelope, I thanked her, and she said, "You might want to check it." She smiled.

I opened it, which I seldom do until I'm home, and the check was for more money than I was owed. Puzzled, I looked up and said, "But this is more than you owe me."

She nodded and smiled again. "We had extra money so we paid you more."

Now, I'm here to tell you—I have *never* had anyone pay me more than they owed. A couple of times, they've paid less but never more.

I learned a lesson about obedience. Also, I was reminded that you cannot outgive God.

I also believe in the tithing of blessings as well as money. Often I'm blessed in a way that has no money attached, but it has enhanced my life and helped me in some way. Whether it's a friend who offers to mow my grass when my mower is in the shop or who runs an errand for me or lends me a lake home or mountain cabin to use as a writing retreat, I see that as a blessing that needs to be tithed back to others. I have learned that the best way to pay back a kindness is to give one away to someone else.

> *The wicked worketh a deceitful work: but to him that soweth righteousness shall be a sure reward. (Proverbs 11:18)*

Another Scripture that refers to sowing is one that has come to have special meaning to me. The night that Mama died, Karen and I went back to my house. I sat down on the sofa, buried my face in my hands, and cried for a minute. I looked up to see my dear friend watching the tears spill down my cheeks.

She smiled sadly, then spoke quietly. "It says in Psalms that those who sow in tears, shall reap in joy."

I knew instantly what the Scripture meant. That if I proclaimed my love and belief in Almighty God at a time when things weren't going my way, then a harvest of happiness and peace would return to me.

> *Weeping may endure for a night, but joy cometh in the morning. (Psalm 30:5)*

I clung to those two Scriptures in those first few days, and they lighted my darkened path. I also heard Mama's words, ones that she had often repeated: "That which don't kill us, makes us stronger."

Yes, it does. Not just in body and mind but, most importantly, in faith. Every opportunity we give him to prove himself faithful and trustworthy allows us to grow stronger to face whatever else comes our way.

Stevie Waltrip has been one of my best friends for over twenty years and is one of the finest women I've ever known. She is a faithful servant of the Lord, an incredible prayer warrior, and the epitome of everything that people love about Southern women. That is to say, she is gracious, hospitable, courteous, lovingly kind, and thoughtful. I am daily inspired by her because she truly seeks the Lord and she genuinely seeks to treat everyone with deep Christian compassion and love. Stevie's not an in-your-face kind of Christian, yet she is deeply resolute in her belief in the Lord and Savior Jesus Christ. She is never timid in standing strong for him and speaking her convictions if asked. Over the years, I have watched many times as she gently stood strong for our heavenly Father and sowed faithfully for him day after day. One day, an unexpected harvest was reaped.

For many years, Stevie had made it a Sunday habit of finding a Scripture for her husband, Darrell Waltrip, the three-time NASCAR champion and Daytona 500 winner. She'd write out the Scripture and then give it to him to tape to the dashboard of his race car. Weekly, he raced with the Lord's words in his wife's handwriting within arm's reach of his steering wheel.

One Sunday as she headed down pit road to give Darrell his Scripture, she ran into Dale Earnhardt who, when he learned what she was doing, demanded—Dale always demanded, never asked—that she do the same for him. In fact, he started by taking Darrell's slip of paper from her and hurrying off to put it on the dashboard of his race car. From that moment on, Stevie found two Scriptures every Sunday morning of race season and gave them to two of the sport's most legendary racers. Dale, of course, got to pick which one he wanted, then gave the other to Darrell.

Fast-forward to February 18, 2001, the day that Darrell began his new career as a race commentator for Fox Sports (which would eventually earn him an Emmy nomination). He had retired from racing, but Stevie was with her husband that morning in Florida, where later in the day the world famous Daytona 500 would take the green flag. That morning, Stevie was sitting on the morning coach, flipping through her Bible, uncertain if Dale would want a Scripture now that Darrell had retired.

"I felt so spiritually dry that morning," Stevie recalled. "I went to the eighteenth chapter of Proverbs because it was the eighteenth day of the month."

As she is always certain to do, Stevie prayed for guidance and asked the Lord to direct her to the Scripture that was right for Dale, the special verse that he needed for that day. She found it, wrote it down, and headed out to pit row, where she found Dale surrounded by a crowd of admirers but eager to receive his Scripture. He read it, hugged her tightly, and proclaimed it to be "perfect."

I don't think anyone knows how the media got hold of that Scripture that was taped to the dashboard of Dale's mangled race car. After his lifeless body was lifted out of the car, safety workers covered it with a tarp, hooked it to a wrecker, and pulled it to a secured area. Still, somehow—I guess by the mightiness of God—the last words that the warrior had read before he entered his last battle was shared, and suddenly it tore through the media like a field on fire. In the days that followed, I read that Scripture in such secular publications as *Time*, *People*, *Sports Illustrated*, and *Newsweek*. It even became an on-air discussion subject for Larry King, who asked Darrell about it a couple of days after the accident. That Scripture would touch thousands of lives and even help some find salvation.

The Scripture that Stevie had given to Dale Earnhardt that day was Proverbs 18:10: "The name of the Lord is a strong tower: the righteous shall runneth into it and are safe."

"You know, Stevie," I said several months later as I sat on a stool in her kitchen as she made coffee, "I think your entire Christian witness has been building toward this one moment in time when you could touch so many lives. It was an innocent gesture and seemed so simple, but it impacted many people."

She stopped at the kitchen sink and turned to look at me with tears glistening in her eyes. She looked as though that had never occurred to her.

"Really?" she asked in a voice of hope. "Do you really think that may have happened?"

I have no doubt. My sweet humble friend, one of God's most faithful, did nothing out of the ordinary on that February day. She simply did what she always does — she spoke up for the Lord, and in doing so, her single voice was heard by a multitude. She sowed and the kingdom of God reaped.

> He which soweth sparingly shall reap also sparingly and he which soweth bountifully shall reap also bountifully. (2 Corinthians 9:6)

Like Stevie, we should all sow daily in our Christian witness because we never know when our big moment is coming, a moment that might seem so small but might go forward to touch hundreds or thousands of people and bring more souls into the heavenly kingdom. Stevie did what she did every day of her life — speak softly but strongly for the Lord — and that tender voice brought an abundance of harvest.

> And herein is that saying true, one soweth and another reapeth. (John 4:37)

Mama B, my brother-in-law's mother, was an amazing Southern woman. She was a beauty queen who also helped to get up hay in the hot summer and clean out chicken houses. No one has ever loved the Lord more, and her witness was always zealous. Whenever she met someone new, her standard barrage of questions were:

"Are you saved?"

"Where do you go to church?"

"Did you go last Sunday?"

"What did the preacher preach on?"

Trust me, no sinner wanted to come within a mile of Mama B for his unsaved soul was not safe from her relentless drive for the redemption of all. But many people have stood up to give their testimony and told how Mama B was the one who witnessed to them and begged them to find the Lord.

One Sunday at church, a man entering the early autumn of his life asked to the join the church based on his declaration of salvation. He told the story that twenty years before Mama B had witnessed to him and led him to accept Christ.

"I got away from him, and I ain't lived like I always should. But I never forgot what she told me and how she led me to Jesus," he said in a quivering voice. "I want to do what's right now and be baptized and become a member of this church."

> And I heard a voice from heaven saying unto me, Write, Blessed are the dead which die in the Lord from henceforth:

*Yea, saith the Spirit, that they may rest from their labors;
and their works do follow them. (Revelation 14:13)*

Sweet Mama B. She soweth for the Lord, and in heaven there is a crown of glory laid up for all her godly labors. The same can be said for us all. For what we sow on this earth, we shall, in all probability, reap on this earth—as well as in glory too.

Chapter 16

THE KINDNESS
OF KINDNESS

After back surgery, my beloved friend Pinky was forced into a transitional-care facility for physical therapy. One day while my dachshund, Dixie Dew, and I were visiting, Pinky took up the subject of being kind. It was something that was heavy on her mind.

In her soft, low drawl, Pinky said, "It's so simple, you know."

"What?"

"'Be ye kind to one another.'" Lying flat in the bed, she stared at the ceiling thoughtfully as she stroked Dixie Dew, lying beside her. "It's one of the first Scriptures I learned as a little girl, but you don't think about it much."

Kindness, genuine and from the heart, is the greatest gift we can give each other, and it is the most wonderful way to serve our good Lord and represent him. In the acts of love that we offer, others will see Christ in us.

"What brought that on?" I asked, puzzled by the conversation's sudden swing.

"I've had nurses who were kind and some who weren't. A kind

word or a pat on the back can make such a difference. It really can. Just be kind."

I nodded. Then a cynicism that I fight back reared its ugly head. "Except if you're building a house. Some contractors don't understand kindness. They understand yelling and meanness."

Building a house and dealing with contractors is another story for another book. This is about kindness. After I left that evening, I thought a great deal about what Pinky, one of the finest Southern women I have ever known, had said. Over the years I have watched Pinky practice an abundance of kindness. There she lay in tremendous pain, and her strongest comfort had come in the form of a nurse's kind words. I can honestly say that I have never witnessed Pinky being unkind or speaking harshly of anyone. Ever. Sometimes I find it frustrating because she guards her words carefully. A not uncommon conversation between us might go like this:

"What did our friend say about not going to that event the other night?" My question broached like that means I think he should have gone.

"I don't know."

"Why don't you know?"

"Because I didn't ask him," she'll reply, shrugging it off.

"Why didn't you ask him?"

"I just didn't." I'll pause dramatically, of course, and then she'll continue. "I just didn't think it was any of my business."

"Pinky, you're useless when it comes to getting the inside story on anything," I'll say with a sigh, and then she'll laugh because she knows she has taken the high road once again.

> *And be ye kind one to another, tenderhearted, forgiving one another, even as God for Christ's sake hath forgiven you. (Ephesians 4:32)*

At the table of hospitality in the South, kindness is the centerpiece filled with bright roses, rich greenery, and fresh baby's breath. The essence of our breed of womanhood is to go out of our way to be kind to others either in word or deed.

"Pretty is as pretty does," our mamas admonish us from the nursery up, reminding us often that beauty lies in how we treat others and not in the creaminess of our complexions or loveliness of our faces. My mama preached "pretty is as pretty does" as often and as stridently as she touted John 3:16. Of course, I welcomed knowing that I could be pretty in actions, since I was so plain in looks. Maybe I wasn't quite "as ugly as homemade sin," a favorite saying of my people and one I never understood, but my chubbiness, freckles, and overbite would never have put me on anyone's list of beauties.

"Why do you suppose that so-and-so didn't do such-and-such?" my sister, Louise, will say from time-to-time, talking about someone who has not responded to kindnesses with similar kindnesses.

"Because not everyone thinks the way we do," I'll reply. "Especially like *you* think."

This is true. There is not a more thoughtful, giving person than Louise. In fact, I think sometimes she takes it to the extreme because she wears herself out with all the good she does.

"There's no one in the world does more for other people than Louise," Mama said often. "She's unreal."

I met a lady once who told me she knew my sister in a passing professional way. The woman said, "Once I went through a terrible time, terrible. Louise heard about it, and though she didn't know me well, she called me up and encouraged me. I'll never forget that."

Dropping these seeds of kindness behind us grows into a lush garden that will spread like kudzu because people often emulate how they are treated. Kindness touches another's heart and makes them more inclined to give to others. Once I went Christmas shopping at my favorite department store in New York City. In the hustle and bustle of the season, the store was packed and the escalator was jammed with a steady stream of people to the point that folks were waiting in line to get on. My turn came, and just as I started to step on, a sullen-looking, attractive blonde woman broke line, pushed me out of the way, and took my place. I was astounded by such rudeness. You would never see that happen at a department store in the South. I was also a bit miffed. It darkened my mood. I rode up the escalator behind her, debating about whether I should say something to her because I thought it would make me feel better. Instead, I bit my tongue and turned my mood around in another way.

In the Christmas shop of the store, I stood in line to buy some ornaments. As the cashier rang up my merchandise, she said perfunctorily, "How are you today?"

I forced a smile. "I'm fine. How are you?"

"Oh, I'm doing okay," she responded as she punched the keys on the register. She stopped and glanced over at the cashier next to her. "I'd be doing better if I could get someone to go and get a peppermint hot chocolate for me." She looked back at me and shook her head. "But no one will go and get me one. Can you believe that?"

I smiled faintly. I wasn't in a good mood, remember? Half-heartedly, I continued the conversation. "No, I can't believe that." I was trying to be amusing, but the tone fell way short. Then, a thought crossed my mind. I had plenty of time until I met my friends, who were shopping elsewhere. I could go and get the peppermint hot chocolate for her. I thought about it.

Finally, I spoke. "Where's the coffee shop?"

She told me and I replied, "I'll go and get it for you."

Now, here's the difference between here and there. Here in the South, such an offer would have been met with much gushing and carrying on. We'd say something like, "You're kiddin' me! You're not serious, are you? You'd really do that for me? Oh my gosh! That's wonderful! Are you sure you don't mind? If it's an imposition, I understand. Really? You don't mind? You're great! Oh thank you so much. Thank you, thank you, thank you! You are so precious!"

But in New York I got this: "Okay. Here's five dollars. That'll cover it."

Off I went, three floors down, bought the peppermint hot chocolate with whipped cream, fought masses on the escalator, and delivered the hot beverage back to the woman. I stepped to the front of the line, apologized to the woman who had just stepped up to pay, and handed the clerk the cup.

The customer tilted her head and looked at me with wonder while the clerk said simply, "Thank you" to me, then to the customer, "I wanted hot chocolate and she offered to go and get it for me."

The woman smiled broadly. The act of kindness had touched her heart, I could see. "How nice!" She studied me for a second, then said, "That was a wonderful thing to do."

I handed the clerk her change, said good-bye, and walked off, in much better spirits than I had been in after the encounter with the rude woman. As I walked away, I heard the clerk say to the customer, "Only someone from the South would have done that. No one here would have ever done that."

Later that afternoon, I had to laugh at how quickly that kindness in the same form was repaid. I got back to the hotel before the others, and while I was waiting for them, I had a sudden and unusual craving for a latte. Out of the blue, my sister walked into the room with a steaming cup in her hand.

"I brought you a latte," she said. Unlike the clerk, though, my thanks was profuse because I was so tickled. The greater gift, though, had come earlier when that small act of kindness had put three of us in a better mood—the other customer, the clerk, and me.

One day Mama had been in the car with me when I drove up to my mailbox and pulled out two armloads of mail. Every day I get an incredible amount of mail. I handed the pile to Mama, who looked at it wistfully and said, "What I'd give to get an armload of mail like this."

What I'd give *not* to get that much, I thought immediately. Wide-eyed and disbelieving, I swung my head around. "Are you serious?"

She nodded solemnly. "It's so lonesome to go to an empty mailbox. Sometimes I'm glad to just get a sales paper."

Gulp.

For those who are widowed, aged, and alone, a note or a card means more than two weeks in Hawaii would mean to my friends. It's something so simple but something that those of us who are blessed with busy lives take for granted.

Her words, so innocent and wistful, shot through my chest, grabbed my heart, and twisted it into such a tangle that it still hasn't straightened out. It reminded me of how we people take for granted those who are older than we are. I wrote a newspaper column about it, and readers responded by emailing to ask for Mama's address so they could send her a card or a note. The response was so heartwarming. One woman in particular, with whom I had worked when I was in college, went the distance. Mary Jo began sending Mama weekly epistles. Sometimes twice a week Mama would happily retrieve a package or an envelope from the mailbox that Mary Jo had sent. The last three years of Mama's life, Mary Jo gave her the greatest kindness —mail for an otherwise empty mailbox.

"She's just made the biggest difference in my life," Mama would often say. "I just love goin' to the mailbox and getting mail!"

Mary Jo's generosity magnified an oft overlooked truth for me—sometimes the most unforgettable kindnesses we can give are to those who aren't overwhelmed with a crowded schedule or a packed mailbox. A note, a visit, or a phone call to those who are shut in, retired, or just plain lonely can fill an empty spot in both their hearts and ours. These moments of kindness are much more important to leave behind than accumulated wealth.

Southerners are exceedingly polite and courteous. Some people like that about us, some people don't. Twice I went out with a guy who had been raised in California and New Jersey. Over lunch one day, he listened intently as I conversed with the waitress. Order completed, she hurried off.

He placed his elbows on the table and leaned closer. "Why are you always so polite to everyone?" He asked the question in a nice but curious way. There was no smart-aleck tone in his voice. He was genuinely perplexed.

I was taken aback and showed it with my wide-eyed expression. "What do you mean?"

"You always call everyone 'ma'am' or 'sir,' and you say 'please' and 'thank you' for everything." He shrugged. "I just find that interesting."

"You don't call people 'sir' or 'ma'am'?" I asked.

"No!" He was emphatic. "And I'm not going to, either. Now, I might call an old man who's ninety years old 'sir,' but I'm not calling anyone else that. No way. They haven't earned my respect. Why would I call a waitress 'ma'am'?"

Now, it was my turn to be floored. The words *sir, ma'am, please, thank you,* and *if you don't mind* are so deeply ingrained in my conscious mind that I use them constantly. Regardless of age, gender, ethnic background, or job status, I speak with courtesy to people. Unless, of course, they have been blatantly rude to me. Then Southern manners are momentarily disposed of.

I studied him for a moment with complete astonishment. "When you were growing up, didn't your mama make you call people 'sir' or 'ma'am'?"

He shook his head vigorously. "No, she didn't. We never had to address people that way. That's one thing I don't understand down here in the South. I like the way people treat me here. It's much nicer and friendlier than up North. But you guys take it too far. Calling someone you don't even know 'ma'am'?" He shook his head again. "That's way too much."

I narrowed my eyes and folded my arms. This is the moment that any glimmer of hope for falling in love died. Right then and there in a Mexican restaurant in Greenville, South Carolina, another budding romance took a nosedive and crashed.

"Well, frankly, I think the least I can do is treat people with courtesy. Especially those who aren't as blessed as I am. Waiting tables is a tough job. The least I can do is to be respectful."

He shook his head and I shook off the possible romance. The Bible says, "Be ye not unequally yoked together with unbelievers." Since he didn't believe in courtesy and respect to all people and I did, we were obviously unequally yoked.

Once, when I was in the painful mode of trying to write by attempting to coax out words lodged stubbornly in my soul, the phone rang.

I welcomed the intrusion.

"Oh, I'm so sorry," a woman wailed sincerely when she heard my voice. "I dialed the wrong number."

I was sorry too. I was hoping for a longer conversation and, therefore, a reprieve from my self-inflicted agony.

"That's perfectly all right," I replied. From the noise level, I could tell she was on a cell phone.

"I was trying to get the bank," she went on to explain. "And I've forgotten the number."

"Which one are you calling?"

She told me, and since it's a bank I use and since I have a good memory, I gave her the phone number.

"Thank you so much! This is wonderful!"

It's also a Southern thing to do because we like to be helpful. It's in our DNA. We're also very friendly. Someone called Mama's house one day when I was there and forty-five minutes later, she hung up the phone. They had talked about, among other things, the weather, traffic, Mama's cold that kept hanging around, and the sale price of fatback at Winn Dixie.

"Who was that?" I asked curiously.

"I don't know. It was a wrong number." She shrugged. "But she was real interesting."

A few days before the lady looking for the bank called, I had dialed a wrong number from my cell phone too and gotten a stranger.

"Wait just a moment, and I'll look the number up for you," the nice woman said.

I love moments like this when I am reminded of the innate goodness of people and how such kindnesses are the normal course of business for those people I proudly call mine. It is people and moments like these that lure others to the sunny graciousness of the South.

Who wouldn't want to live among people like us!

One evening in Mama's kitchen, I noticed a calendar that charts the cycles of the moon and, therefore, is filled with lots of good information about the best time for planting, harvesting, weeding, and various surgeries. I didn't know how she got it, but it had been distributed by a funeral home about sixty miles away. I called and the funeral director answered. I asked about the calendars.

"Just got some in this week," he replied. "Stop by and get 'cha one."

"I would but I live an hour away."

"Then, I'll mail it to you."

"Really? I'll send a check for the postage." I couldn't believe that someone would go to the trouble and expense, especially for someone who won't be using their business. After all, everyone knows you have to use a funeral home close to where you live because your friends will travel only so far to see you after you're dead and gone.

"I'll put it in the mail first thing tomorrow. Ain't no charge. Happy to do it, ma'am. Stop in and visit with us when you're over in our neck of the woods."

And sure enough, a few days later, the calendar arrived and with it another warm reminder of old-fashioned goodness. Maybe it's not in style like it used to be, but I sure like the way that such old-fashioned goodness fits. Just like a fleece-lined sweatshirt on a cool autumn morning, small kindnesses feel cozy and perfect and are perfect examples of Christian love.

> She openeth her mouth with wisdom; and in her tongue is
> the law of kindness. (Proverbs 31:26)

Like Pinky reminded me that day, a kind word or action is the greatest gift we can give one another.

Chapter 17

DO GOOD
UNTO OTHERS

ack in the "politically incorrect" days of my childhood—when school children were allowed to pray each morning, say the Pledge of Allegiance, and sing "Dixie"—our teachers as well as our parents taught us the Golden Rule: Do Unto Others As You Would Have Them Do Unto You.

You could also call this the rule of discipline because every time a child misbehaved, the adult applying the discipline would quote it then say, "Now, is this the way you would like for Neal to treat you?"

It worked. It still works. That piece of wisdom, not surprisingly, comes from a Biblical command in Matthew: "Therefore all things whatsoever ye would that men should do to you, do ye even so to them" (7:12).

Every morning, our grade school teacher would bring class to order, call the roll, then command that we stand and pledge allegiance to the flag. We slid out of our desks, the ones with the seat attached to the desk, which had a lid that could be raised for storage.

Proud and erect, our heads held high, we placed our small hands over our hearts and swore devotion to the United States of America, one nation under God. Now, some claim that's politically incorrect, as well as a breach of our Constitutional instructions. They want those four words taken out of the pledge — "one nation under God." As an elementary student, I took those words for granted. Said them automatically. But now, I take them to heart, and I take umbrage to anyone who says we should discard them.

Then there's the matter of the Lord's Prayer, which we also said every morning, immediately after the Pledge of Allegiance. That's right. Some say that's politically incorrect too and a breach of separation of church and state, but, by golly, we did it. Right there, out in the open. We prayed. And had we refused to pray or pledge the flag, Mrs. Chambers, Mrs. Rudeseal, or Mrs. Satterfield would have marched, in those pointy-toed high heels they all wore, right up and grabbed the offender's hand and smacked it hard with a twelve-inch ruler. Hand-smacking with a ruler too is politically incorrect in today's environment.

My grammar school, a one-story brick building with a half basement and old wood floors that always smelled of oil and disinfectant, housed grades one through six. The first four grades were on one end and the last two on the other end, separated by an auditorium and the principal's office. Our principal, Mr. Cronic, was a spirit-called layman preacher. Because of that, and because he was unencumbered by any disapproving school board, Mr. Cronic sought to instill in us proper Christian values. Just in case, some of us weren't getting it at home.

Once a month, a Bible storyteller came and entertained us from the creaky stage of that old auditorium, with the heavy, dark red-velvet curtains that hung to the side. I can see her now. Though I have long forgotten her name, I remember exactly how she looked. She was a large-boned woman, maybe six feet tall, with wide shoulders and short, fine light brown hair. Her storytelling was magical, whether she told of the Good Samaritan, Jesus' birth, or Moses and the Ten Commandments, she weaved a story that was enchanting. Just as we got breathlessly into the story, she stopped it and said, "Next month we'll pick up right there and find out what happened when Delilah cut off all of Samson's hair."

We hated for the story to end, but we looked forward to the next month when she would come again. I believe that she probably even had a story about the Golden Rule.

I also had a set of albums that played on those little, now-old-fashioned turntables. The records were filled with children's stories that had a moral to them. Always one to love good storytelling then as now, I would put one on the turntable every night, turn the lights off, crawl into bed, and listen to the characters act out a story in which a child was always put into a situation of choosing between right and wrong. The needle would play across the record, and when it reached the end, the needle would lift and return to its resting position, leaving my somber soul filled with good teachings as I drifted off to sleep.

As childhoods go, mine was sweet in a typically Southern way. It was filled with church — lots of church — family dinners, backyard swings, mud pies, and summer afternoons spent splashing in the swimming hole as the boys grabbed a rope tied to a tall oak tree and soared out over the deepest part of the river, dropping with an explosion of splashing water and noise.

I've always loved and cherished my childhood, which is why it is terribly sad — a rude awakening really — to discover my picturesque Southern childhood was politically incorrect. Or so says some.

One day, I was having lunch after church with Pinky, who is a retired school teacher. Never will you find a woman more dedicated to her faith and witnessing in a subtle way than Miss Pinky. Loving the Lord and serving him with daily acts of kindness has always been her way. Now, back to the days when teachers were allowed to let their faith show in the classroom, Pinky had an annual habit of buying New Testaments for her fourth grade class when the school year ended. Each year, she handed out little red New Testaments to each student, some of whom had never been in church.

That day at lunch, a young man, dressed in suit and tie, approached our table. "Hello, Mrs. Cabe," he greeted her with a sweet smile. He was holding a toddler in his arms, and by his side was a lovely, obviously adoring wife.

After niceties were exchanged, the young man said, "Mrs. Cabe, I want you to know that I'm a minister now, and it all started with you. Remember those little red Testaments you used to give us?" She nodded quietly, and he continued. "Thanks to you and what you taught us in the fourth grade, more than just writing and arithmetic, I found the Lord and my calling. Thank you so much."

Tears filled my eyes, and I bit my lip to keep from letting them spill down my face. Pinky, in her simple way of serving the Lord daily, had impacted many lives, including many she would never know, like the folks that the young minister would help to bring into the Lord's Kingdom.

"Wow, Pinky," I mumbled softly when the young man walked away. "That's powerful. Think of all the good you've done with those little red Testaments."

In typical fashion, she shrugged it off and said humbly, "It wasn't much. I just did what I could until things changed and they wouldn't let me do it anymore."

I believe that I know wrong from right, but there are times when a gray area invades and I'm not quite sure. When that happens, I do one of two things: I call a trusted friend for Christian counsel, or I ask myself how would the Golden Rule play out here?

That simple childhood teaching is the core of my adult behavior. Funny, isn't it?

Sadly, some of the meanest people can sometimes be Christians who proclaim themselves to be enforcers of all things biblical. They mean well. They believe they're standing up for God, and heaven knows we need more people to stand up for him. But when we judge or criticize other Christians, we fail our Lord by not forgiving and loving. As those around me often say, "Love the sinner. Hate the sin." As Daddy always said, "There are no big sins and little sins. Sin is sin."

One thing that troubles me greatly are folks who will use my Christian beliefs against me. In other words, they try to manipulate me using Scriptures and my faith as weapons to fight me. I believe this is something we all face, so I share it to warn you of this: do what the Lord expects of you, but don't let the enemy use your beliefs in a way that takes away what is yours.

I've had people who wrote me bad checks—sometimes from book sales at church events—and when I tried to collect, those people thought I should forgive the debt I was owed because it would be "the Christian thing to do." Once, a woman who was infringing on a trademark that I own—and had spent years and a good bit of money in obtaining—balked at a request to quit using it by sending me a Scripture invoking me to live in peace with all, whenever possible. I had been very courteous and respectful when I had approached these people about resolving these issues, yet they tried to win the battle by playing the Christian card on me. Both were in the wrong, going against biblical teachings, yet they wanted me to overlook that and let them cheat me because my faith should allow them to do that.

Yes, I'm a Christian but that doesn't give anyone the right to steal from me, cheat me, or kill me. Southern women are often feisty and strong spirited. We believe that what's right is right and what's wrong is wrong. If you scorn us or one of our family members, we'll fight. It's okay to stand up against wrong when you do it courteously and with respect.

Once, a church booked me to speak for an event. Over the months leading up to the event, I turned down four other engagements for that same night. About two weeks before the event, someone from the church called and said, "We're so sorry, but we have to cancel. There's another event in town that many of our members are going to, so we won't have the crowd we expected."

My heart sank and my mouth went dry. I had turned down four other offers for that night, so I would be out the income. Two events had even offered a good bit more money, but I had honored my commitment to the church. I explained that to her and said, "So, y'all will just have to pay me anyway." This is standard in the speaking business; when someone is obligated for a date, the host will usually honor the fee if it's canceled.

"Well," she began worriedly. "We'll send you what we have, but our women's group doesn't have that much."

I was nice but firm. "Then you'll have to borrow from the church." She didn't say anything, and I continued. "I honored my commitment to you even when I was offered more money, and I know you'll want to do what's right."

What could she say to that?

She called back shortly and said they would pay the fee. "If you're going to do that, why not just have the event?" I asked. They did and they made enough money to cover all expenses. In the end, we all won. But if I had not stood up for myself, I would have lost out. As Christians, we have the right to stand up for ourselves—even against other Christians.

Sunday school, church, grade school, and those storytelling records gave me a strong, solid idea of the right way to treat other people as well as myself. I like for a situation to be fair to both sides, and since I'm usually one of those sides, I want it to be fair to me.

Yes, there are times when we have to be emotionally big and walk away from situations. Sometimes we're tested by our heavenly Father, and we have to take it on the chin. We know when those times are because we feel it with a heaviness in our spirit. It's against what the flesh wants, but we know—we just *know*—what we should do. Still, no Christian should be expected to lie down and let others walk on her time after time. Respect yourself, the other person, and the good Lord by how you stand up for yourself. Being a Christian doesn't mean we have to walk around with a big sign on our foreheads that says, "I'm a Christian. Feel free to take advantage of me." Not at all.

Do Unto Others As You Would Have Done Unto You: that's still the golden rule of conduct. Do that, then expect others to do unto you as they would have done unto themselves. It's a reasonable expectation. If it doesn't seem fair, ask the other person, "Is this how you would want to be treated in this situation?"

I think often of a couple who were divorcing after many years of marriage and after building a hugely successful business. They had started from scratch, worked side-by-side, and built an enormous national business. Negotiations for the split of the business and personal properties dragged on quite some time. Finally, the judge asked them to each bring a proposed settlement on what each felt was fair. At the next hearing, the wife presented her proposal then the husband presented his. Immediately, the judge could see that the wife was being reasonable and fair but the husband was not.

"Do you really believe this is an equitable settlement for your wife?" the judge asked.

"Yes sir. Completely," the husband answered and expounded on why it was so good.

"Hmm," the judge pondered it a bit. "Would you be happy if this were your settlement?"

"Absolutely."

"Great," the judge replied. "Then I'm taking your proposed settlement, and I'm awarding what you think you should keep to your wife and what you think your wife should have to you. I think you'll be very happy with it since you believe it's so fair."

True story. That's how the wife wound up owning the entire business they had built together.

The moral is simple. In every situation, there is a judge — and there really is one — who can turn the tables on you and give you what you're giving to others. The Golden Rule is still golden. Do good unto others and good will come back unto you.

Chapter 18

SITTING UP WITH THE DEAD

When Mama had open-heart surgery a few years ago, her doctors warned her of the risk of death because of her advanced age. The surgeon, standing by her hospital bed, watched closely for her reaction.

Mama, undeterred by his warning, simply shrugged, took another bite of applesauce, and replied casually, "Fine. Go ahead and do it."

Since Daddy died, she had talked often of him and her other loved ones waiting for her on the other side.

"I've got just as many over there as I've got here. They're waitin' for me in heaven, and I'm lookin' forward to goin'."

On the morning of the surgery, I followed the gurney down the sterilized white hallways until we reached the double doors of the operating room. There, one of the orderlies said, "This is as far as you can go."

We had already prayed before we left the room, so Mama took my hand, kissed it, and smiled sweetly. "Now don't worry. No matter what happens, I'm a winner either way."

My mama was absolutely fearless of death. She had no qualms or hesitations. On earth, my mama was more dependent than independent, always counting on the rest of us to take care of her. She refused to go anywhere by herself and would not, at any urging, walk into a room by herself. Someone always had to be by her side. Yet there was no shyness in stepping toward what most people fear the most. She steadfastly believed that life eternal in a better place awaited her and that she would rejoin those she loved who had gone before. She talked about it easily, comfortably, and, to me, too often.

"I want to see your daddy again and be with the Lord."

"Oh Mama, don't talk that way. I think you can live to be ninety-five or a hundred," I said, almost pleading.

I believed that too, because she was in such great health, so young-acting and vibrant.

"I don't want to live that long. I can't live forever." Her tone was casual and common-sensical. "I'm ready to go home just as soon as the Lord calls me."

To my people, because of our steadfast faith and our belief in eternal life, we have never shrunk back from death. No, we don't exactly run toward it, but we don't run away from it. Southerners are comfortable with the concept of death because our people believe that in a twinkling of an eye, we will pass from this life into the presence of our Holy Lord and know sweet life everlasting.

Probably in no other region of the United States do folks talk as effortlessly and comfortably of death as we do in the South. We often talk among ourselves of what we want at our funerals and about that glorious day when we find ourselves at the Pearly Gates.

The aunt of a friend of mine spends much of her time these days planning her funeral. Whenever a preacher makes her mad, she scratches his name off the list of those eulogizing her and adds the name of whichever one is in her favor. Every time she buys a new dress, she'll hold it up in front of her, look in the mirror, and ask whoever is with her, "How would I look laid out in this?"

She has precisely instructed that she is to be adorned in one dress for the visitation, then her body is to be changed into a red dress—red is her favorite—for burial.

"Why, Aunt Mary, whoever heard of changing clothes on the deceased?" my friend asked.

Aunt Mary drew herself up tall and sharpened her voice. "I don't care who does it or who don't! But it'll be done for me. Of that, I can assure you."

"Why?" My friend couldn't leave it alone.

"Because anyone who knows me knows I'd *never* wear the same dress two days in a row!"

<hr />

After attending two funerals within a course of a few days, my sister and I had had plenty of time to critique the eulogies, flowers, and general overall presentation of the home-going events. That's what my daddy always called it when folks passed from here to there—*home-going*. Each time he prayed publicly, he always said, "Please, Lord God, be with those who are heartsick over the home-going of loved ones." For those who are destined for heaven, there is simply no better way to say it. Home-going.

At both funerals, Louise and I sat quietly in our best black dresses and cut our eyes over at each other in disapproval when the preachers' eulogies had stretched into sermons of salvation and the need for such if one expected to make it to heaven when death summoned. Now, we're all for salvation. We believe in it strongly, you know, but funerals, or so we believe, should be about the person who died. A celebration of the life departed, a temporary reprieve for preachers looking to gather lost souls into the fold. It is only befitting.

At the meal that followed the second funeral, my brother-in-law, Rodney, and I were munching on a plate full of various salads, casseroles, and desserts when Louise came charging up to us, full of purpose. It was written all over her face.

"I'm telling you." She pointed at me. "And I'm telling you." She pointed at Rodney.

I held up my hand to stop her. "I'm telling you too. I agree completely."

Rodney looked first at me, then at Louise, and then shook his head in bewilderment. "You two are crazy." He turned to me. "How do you even know what she's talking about?"

I ignored him and continued the conversation with my sister. "When I die, you make sure my funeral is about *me*."

"Exactly!" she exclaimed.

"Don't let 'em preach salvation at my funeral," I continued. "I want my funeral to be about me. *All about me*."

"I agree completely," she nodded vigorously. "Promise me the same thing. Find people who will talk about how wonderful I was." Then she suggested a couple of folks.

Of course, we were mostly kidding. But not completely.

I remember as a child when folks still sat up with the dead. Taking them home was a way of life back then, and folks often peppered their stories by saying something like, "I seen him the other night when Elmer lay a corpse."

As best I can tell, this tradition started back in the nineteenth century when the dead were laid out on beds, awaiting the pine boxes that were being built. You see, the folks, without many doctors in the rural areas, weren't always sure that the dead were really dead. Perhaps they were merely slumbering deeply or in a coma, so they wanted to make sure they were dead and gone before boxing them up. And sometimes, the dead did rise up, not resurrected mind you, but merely renewed from a refreshing sleep.

The tradition then carried through into the twentieth century because funeral homes were often just one or two small rooms where technicalities were performed. There was not room to host a viewing.

But even after funeral homes grew in space, folks often continued to take their beloved ones home, wishing to bid them farewell in the bosom of hearth and family.

Though that tradition has passed away now, there is one that remains strong with my people, and that is the habit of talking about heaven in terms of calling it "home."

"When I get home, I'm gonna ask the Lord why he didn't let it rain that summer when all the crops died. I'll be mighty interested to hear his reasoning for it," someone is apt to say.

Though I was tiny, I can remember, albeit a bit faintly, trailing along with my parents to visit homes and pay respects to the departed and his family. I recall caskets tucked away in the corner of a living room or in front of a big picture window, and I can recall the smell of carnations that permeated the air.

The two scenes I recall most vividly both involved mothers crazed with grief over the loss of their sons. It is something that no matter how tender the young age, you never forget.

The little abode was really a shack. To call it anything else would embellish and gloss over the crippling humbleness of the family that occupied its four tiny rooms with its ragged porch that barely hung onto its tar paper front. The boy was seventeen, killed when his car took a deep curve too fast. They took him home to mourn him, taking down the Christmas tree so they could squeeze the coffin into the little room.

His mama's wails still haunt me today.

When my parents built their house in 1957, my daddy had been firm in his instructions. "Make that front door big enough to bring a casket in through it."

We only used it once. When I was six and my baby nephew died of instant pneumonia at six months old, breaking the hearts of his parents and mine. I remember that tiny casket in front of the picture window, a handsome baby in a blue sweater outfit and his beautiful mother who screamed in agony as she crumbled to the floor.

There are some things that, no matter how you try to escape them, will pry themselves deep into your memory and there remain for the rest of your days.

It is not certain how we got on the subject, but somehow a friend mentioned that when he dies, he wants "What a Wonderful World" by Louis Armstrong to be played at his funeral.

"I want people to laugh and be happy at my funeral," he said, as if that is even a remotely normal thought. I rolled my eyes.

Though that's one of my favorite songs, I couldn't imagine any such. Nor do I want it. I made a face and shook my head at such a disdainful thought.

"Not me," I declared empathically. "I want there to be great wailing and weeping and gnashing of teeth when I die. I want people lying prostrate with grief across my casket."

He chuckled. "Somehow that doesn't surprise me."

"Truly," I continued in all seriousness, "I want it to be a pitiful, moaning display of sorrowful mourning."

"I'll remember that, and if you go before me—hopefully, it won't be for many years—I'll be sure to display the appropriate amount of weeping and wailing at your funeral."

"And gnashing of teeth," I reminded him.

"Oh yes, and gnashing of teeth. I promise."

"And make sure that others act appropriately sorrowful. I'll give you a list of who needs to be the most laden with grief."

Well, really, who wants people laughing when they're gone? That would mean that they're happy that this world is no longer graced with your presence and that life is made better by death's summons. Still, I have known a couple of people who passed from this world and there was silent rejoicing over those departures.

A while back, an old man I knew died, and many considered it to be a cleansing of evil in this world. No one could recall a moment of kindness as he had drifted, grumbling, through our lives.

"There goes the meanest man the good Lord ever blew breath in," I mumbled, quoting Calpunia from *To Kill A Mockingbird* when she watches the body of Boo Radley's father carried from his house.

Others agreed, and it became a discussion of how mean, ornery, and downright despicable he had been. Stories were told of how he lied, cheated, and tricked.

"He's gonna bust the gates of hell wide open," someone predicted.

"Well, maybe he made things right in the end," another demurred sweetly. Southerners always want to believe the best about death and those who have succumbed to its demand.

"Not likely. He made his deal with the devil a long time ago. It was a brotherhood of demons." Guess who said that?

Since my dear friend Karen is a gospel singer, constantly traveling for concerts and shows, I thought I should find out exactly where I stand with her.

"If I died and you had a show date somewhere, would you do the show or come to my funeral?"

I'm happy—and a bit surprised—to report there was no hesitation. "Why I absolutely would be at your funeral!" she exclaimed resolutely. "I'd either cancel the date or get someone to go for me."

"Really?" I grinned broadly.

"Without question," she assured me. "Absolutely."

Now, I'm really relieved because I know that if Karen is going to be there, I can count on a significant amount of mournful sorrow and uncontrolled weeping. Some, though, leave this world and all that lingers is the collective sigh of those who feel unburdened. There are a few who can bring more joy to people by dying than by living. Yes, I know I'll be with Jesus when I'm gone, but there still needs to be some sorrow on this earth over my departure for heaven.

So please, when I'm gone, let there be no rejoicing or joy of spirit. I've got all my hopes pinned on huge displays of wailing, gnashing of teeth, and bone-deep sorrow.

Plenty of it too, if you would be so kind.

Chapter 19

COME YE HEAVY LADEN
AND I WILL GIVE YOU REST

Many times Mama would say to me, after we had prayed our way through yet another crisis, either minor or major, "What do folks do when they don't have the Lord to help 'em through?"

My answer, quiet and thoughtful, was always the same: "I don't know." I can't imagine a life where the good Lord is not a constant companion, a life where I couldn't take my concerns, requests, or troubles to a greater power that cares and comforts. I think I'd surely lose my mind.

"Pray about it and leave it in the Lord's hands," Daddy always instructed. Over the years I have tried, but many are the times that I have thought that the good Lord could certainly use my help. As he has often reminded me: he doesn't.

During my time on earth, I have seen many storms of life, both those where I watched as an observer, like one watches a movie, and those where I was given either a starring or co-starring role. If troubles are truly our greatest teacher, then the strongest lesson I have learned is simple: find the Lord *before* you need him. I have watched as people, who had never sought the Lord in good and prosperous times, cried out for a God that was distant and a stranger to them when troubles came calling. I have also seen people whose relationship with Jesus Christ was close and intimate, so much so that when those horrendous storms came, they merely raised a hand toward the heavens and said, "Dear Lord, take my hand and hold it tightly until these storms pass. Be with me until the waters are calm again."

For all my experience on this earth, I can tell you, it is better to be in the latter category than the first. Until the day I pass from here unto glory, I shall never forget that summer morning, as the sun rose bright and beautiful, streaming its golden rays through the plate-glass windows of the waiting room of the hospital emergency area. The doctor had been gentle and kind, but his words were unintentionally harsh, bringing forth unrelenting agony for some. He told a young man that his daddy had died. The young man, a Christian for only two years, who had been brought up in a home of religious renegades, dropped to his knees and cried woefully, "Dear God, please don't send my daddy to hell! Please dear God, don't let him go to hell." It was one of the most heart-wrenching moments of my life.

But the eternal destination had been his father's choice, and wherever he went when death summoned, there was no changing it by those left behind. Until the day I watched my mama die, I had no true understanding of what the Bible calls "in the twinkling of an eye." But now forever more, I shall know how quickly that is. Mama stood in the foyer of my home, laughing. She tossed a finger at me—Mama was the greatest user of the forefinger of anyone ever—winked, and said, "And don't you forget that." Then the aneurysm burst in her head, she fell over, tumbled down the step into my sunken living room, and Mama, the woman who had prayed for me, cried for me, and believed always in me, was gone. In the all-too-brief twinkling of an eye. From that moment forward I knew that would be an important part of my testimony: don't wait to find the Lord, because death can come so quickly, so unexpectedly, that salvation that has not already been gained can be lost forever.

A standard bluegrass music favorite is a song called "Man of Constant Sorrow," which regained renewed popularity in the hit movie *O Brother, Where Art Thou?* Written decades ago by country singer Arthur Emery, it expressed how the people of the Southern mountains felt during the Depression—sorrow was a constant companion. The wisest of Southern women have learned that sorrow is the greatest teacher in our lives. Sorrow teaches while laughter amuses. It's that simple.

Sorrow and laughter can be compared to parents. Sorrow takes on the traditional role of the father—stern, disciplined, and teaching though it hurts. Laughter is the mother that loves, hugs, and soothes. We need both, for our lives will not be balanced or reach full potential without them. When we are sorrowful or burdened with hard times, we are reflective and constantly seeking guidance. We probe and try to figure out the equation. By examining the problem or hurt from every angle, we gain wisdom. Throughout the book of Proverbs, one message rises repeatedly: Get knowledge and understanding. Also, adversity tests our character as people and as Christians. It is through the difficult times—when we have to truly lean on the Lord and cast our cares on him—that our faith grows.

As one of my dear girlfriends, Gregg, reminds me, "The Bible says *when* trouble comes, not *if.*"

> *These things I have spoken unto you, that in me ye might have peace. In the world ye shall have tribulation: but be of good cheer; I have overcome the world. (John 16:33)*

The faith of our foremothers, strengthened by the many hardships they faced, have taught us that not only are we strengthened by challenges but so is our relationship with God. Trust in the Lord is built when we cannot manage things ourselves and must call on him. Unfortunately, too often we only do that when we have no other choice. Though God would like to be our first choice, he won't turn his back on us even when we make him our last choice.

Southern women often have an admirable attitude about trouble and sorrow: "The good Lord will see us through and make something great out of it."

"What the enemy means for our harm, the Lord will turn to our good" is an ancient belief we often share with each other during these challenges.

When I am burdened and heavy laden, I often say aloud—sometimes through anguished tears—"Lord, I just can't wait to see what good you bring out of this. Because I know it's going to be something great." Those words—spoken out loud—lift my spirits and give me the encouragement to plow on through. I know my Lord won't let me down.

During painful times, I often take comfort in words I found in Ecclesiastes 7:3: "Sorrow is better than laughter: for by the sadness of the countenance, the heart is made better."

My own pain has made me more compassionate toward others who suffer. Through my empathy, I am able to genuinely reach out to more people. Southern women always believe in looking up and reaching out by finding the best to glean from each situation. I often find myself inspired by other Southern women who lift their chin defiantly in the face of heartbreak and carry on. One of the bravest women I've ever witnessed was Janice, whose daughter, Selena, married my nephew Rod.

For months, everyone had been excitedly planning the spring nuptials. Janice's husband, Kenneth, by the accounts of those who knew best, wasn't a man to be excited easily, but just mention his daughter's wedding and his eyes blazed with happiness and anticipation. Whenever I think of how God's plans can override ours, I think of those wedding plans. Nine days before the sweet event, Kenneth disappeared. Without a trace, without a clue, without a word to anyone. Kenneth was gone. Forty-eight hours later, a park ranger found him in his pickup near a river where he had gone to spend an afternoon fishing. At forty-six years old, his heart had suddenly, unexpectedly sputtered its way to its last beat.

It goes without saying that his family, especially his wife, was devastated.

As plans began for his funeral, the big question became, "Should we postpone the wedding next week?"

Through her tears and her sorrow, Janice was adamant. "Absolutely not. He was looking forward to this wedding so much, and if we postponed it, he would be so mad."

On Monday, Janice, completely grief stricken, buried her husband. Then, she put her pain aside to finish preparations for Saturday's big wedding. On Wednesday, she stood in rain and mud to direct the crew who was raising the huge white tent for the reception. She checked final details such as menus, dresses, and flowers.

Then the day arrived; the day that the family both welcomed and dreaded. It would be a day of both celebration and mourning.

A packed church of well-wishers turned to watch Janice, beautiful in both face and spirit, cling to the arm of her son and walk the aisle to her seat. She walked tall and proud with her head held high, a smile glistening on her face. Not once, did her lip quiver or her eyes moisten.

It was the most gorgeous example of a Steel Magnolia that I have ever witnessed.

Not one tear dropped from her eyes. But many dripped from the eyes of those who watched. We could not fathom what she was feeling. We could not believe the privilege we had of seeing bravery at its best. The seat next to her was empty, and she was alone. Still, there was no self-pity.

"I was determined that the day was going to be about Selena," she said later. "This was her wedding and I refused to let my broken heart overshadow her happiness."

That is unconditional love at its most potent.

It makes me mighty proud to know that the blood of that remarkable woman has now mixed with the blood of my people, for you can never have too much steel in your magnolias. I can now say that I have lived long enough to see unconditional love go eyeball to eyeball with life at its most cruel, and that I have watched as God poured strength into a broken vessel and made it strong. It is a sight that engraves itself in your soul—for it cannot be forgotten. Nor should it ever be.

It makes me think of what my good friend, Norman, a stupendous newspaper man, once told me: "People compare Southern women to steel magnolias but they're more like weeping willows. No matter how much you bend 'em, you can't break 'em."

When difficult times happen, we have basically two choices. We can fight God, which immediately and ultimately gets us nowhere. We can just blow up and pitch an all-out conniption fit, the kind of emotional disturbance made famous by the women of the South. After all, there's an art to pitching a conniption fit. Or we can make the better choice: we can figuratively crawl into God's lap and say, "I don't understand and I hurt, but I love you anyway. Please give me comfort."

I've tried both. And my experience has been that the last way gets me further. With the first, time gets stuck in a place of dismal disappointment until I accept it and can then move forward. With the second choice, God comes immediately to give me comfort. And while he can't give back that which is gone permanently, as in the death of loved ones, he can give me other blessings. When I had suffered great personal loss in the casualties of people I love enormously, I, in the tradition of my people, soldiered on. Spiritually, I was strong, but that was the only place where I had sufficient strength. Mentally, my mind seemed often to hit the pause button and stick. Emotionally, I was tender, and physically, the back-to-back shocks had stretched my nerves to the nth degree.

I felt like a rubber band that was stretched as far as it could go, so I was either going to break or go back to normal. I knew, absolutely knew, that God would not let me break, that he would gently ease me back to my original shape. I trusted him. While he could not give me back what was gone for good in this life, he could give me other blessings, and he did. Those blessings brought comfort while I also relied on a peace that surpasses all understanding. When you know the Lord, you can find that peace over devastation during times of heartbreak. I speak from too much personal experience.

> Come unto me, all ye that labor and are heavy laden, and
> I will give you rest. Take my yoke upon you, and learn of
> me; for I am meek and lowly in heart: and ye shall find rest
> unto your souls. For my yoke is easy, and my burden light.
> (Matthew 11:28–30)

Moments after Mama died, my sister, Louise, was ravaged with grief and was crying hard, recalling our brother's death a few weeks before. "How will I ever make it through this?" she asked. "First, Randall and now Mama. How will I make it?" Louise, firm in her Christian belief, was momentarily sideswiped by the shock. Deep down, she had the secret to survival. Her best friend, Tammy, though, stepped forward. She too had faced great loss when her teenage daughter was taken in a car accident. Tammy smiled broadly and said firmly, "I'll tell you how—through the grace of God. He'll see you through!"

Through my tears, I smiled and went over and hugged her. "Honey, there's not another person in this room who could say that with greater authority." The Lord had brought her through the storms of loss, and he was ready and willing to do the same for us.

And he did.

Chapter 20

THE AMEN CORNER

There is no denying that there was a period — its length stretched well past a hundred years — when the people of the Southern mountains struggled mightily to secure a meager existence. Photographs of that time show somber faces with nary a smile but eyes that seem to be etched not with bitterness or malice but with hope and optimism. Faith ran so deep through this line of stubborn people that the devil couldn't wrestle it away from them and lack of food could not starve them out of it.

"There's a better day a-comin'," said one to another often. For they always believed — always — in a better day, either here in this life or there on the other side where angels sing in harmony and streets are paved with gold.

> *[Jesus said,] "In my father's house are many mansions. If it were not so, I would have told you. I go to prepare a place for you." (John 14:3)*

In one of the many well-worn Bibles that Daddy left behind for those who descended from his loins, he marked with little stars chapter 21 of Revelation, beginning with verse 16. It's where John saw the city of New Jerusalem—the heaven that awaits for those who believe. In detail, John describes the streets of pure gold, walls of jasper, foundations garnished with precious stones, and gates of solid pearl.

My daddy, like those of our people before us, believed that this earth is merely a stopping-off place on a journey toward glory untold. Though he was a man who rarely marked in his Bible, he had specifically denoted that Scripture so he could return to it time after time and be reminded of what lay ahead for him.

Deeply embedded in the South for many generations were people who would not only define the steadfast faith of that region but would come to represent strongly the core of the Bible Belt. Up from the midst of these people arose a remarkable breed of women. They were, in a very lovely sense of the word, feminist before such a term was coined. It began with the Civil War, a time that would see our women marry their indomitable spirits and keen resourcefulness with physical labor and independence. When the men left their farms and towns to do battle, our women on the home front stayed to fight for survival. They sowed fields and reaped harvests, repaired roofs that leaked, hauled water from the creeks, tended to their families, and worried about taxes that had to be paid. And through it all, they prayed.

When the war ended, the men who lived to return to their families would find a different kind of woman awaiting, one who had been forged by the firestorms of adversity. This baptism by fire would create a woman who would never again be backed down by life, no matter how severe. A century later, folks would call these kinds of women "feminist," but through the years, we have simply called them "typical" of Southern feminine upbringing. We believe heartily in defying tribulation, denying pessimism, and denouncing nay-sayers who underestimate our abilities. It comes down to faith in our Lord and faith in ourselves, a potent combination. Our women, centered in this faith, would become underpinning support beams in the churches in which they congregated. If men are the self-appointed head of the body of Christ, then women are undeniably the heart. It is the heart that allows the church to function with compassion and love, two of the most important teachings of Jesus and his servant Paul.

Much ado is made by some about the apostle Paul's admonishments for women to be quiet in church while men preach and run things. Like many Southern Christians, I believe in the undefiled Word of God, which means I adhere to it as it is written. Still, I firmly believe in women who are anointed to be about God's business and to serve him faithfully in various ways. The apostle Paul himself wrote of several women who were of enormous importance to him during the early days of the church and pointed out how his work could not have been completed without the service of Priscilla, Lydia, Lois, Eunice, and others. From the beginning to the end of the Scriptures, we find women who were given missions—Sarah, Esther, Ruth, Naomi, Elizabeth, Martha, and, of course, Mary, the mother of Christ.

Until recent years, there was a corner reserved for men in smaller Southern churches. It was called "the Amen Corner." These men were the pillars of the church—deacons and other preachers. Many times, you often heard "Amen, brother!" rise up from those hallowed benches as they supported the sermon that filtered across the congregation from the pulpit. Somehow, maybe it's the changing of the times, the Amen Corner has passed away in most churches. It isn't, by any stretch of the imagination, that a man's role in the church has lessened, but rather that women are receiving more credit and admiration for their vital roles. This is a good thing. After all, if it hadn't been for Eve, there would have been no population because there would not have been childbirth (remember the curse she was given), and without Mary, there would not have been the greatest birth of all. Come to think about it, we women have been way underestimated for way too long when it comes to the church.

One Sunday morning I was visiting a church where a quick discussion took place between the hymns about an upcoming fellowship lunch to be served a couple of weeks later. A large, formidable, no-nonsense woman stood up in the choir loft and said, "Now every time we have one of these fellowship dinners, it's us women who wind up with all the work—we cook, serve, and clean up. How 'bout you guys helpin' us out a bit?" She narrowed her eyes and scanned the audience for the men. "Let's put some 'fellow' in this fellowship business."

The other women broke into applause, I laughed, and the men turned red. Two weeks later, I returned for the fellowship dinner to find that her words had fallen on deaf ears. Not one man offered to lift a hand to clean up. And worse than that, the church doesn't even have an automatic dishwasher!

In the South, Baptist churches typically have a summer revival that includes seven straight nights of services, and some of the smaller churches even host morning worships as well. The Methodists are a bit smarter. They have their revivals at campgrounds where families "tent" in little rough-shod houses, shaded by massive oaks and maples. Many of these simple little houses—some even have pine straw on the floors—have been passed down through a hundred years of family. They make it a week of visiting, eating plenty, and relaxation.

We Baptists are more of the sackcloth-and-ashes kind when it comes to summer revival. We go to the church house, sit on the hard benches, and if the churches don't have air conditioning, we fan ourselves briskly with funeral-home fans. These are pieces of cardboard attached to thin wooden sticks, which usually have one of two pieces of artwork on them: Jesus knocking at a door that has no outside knob on it or Jesus holding the little lamb that left the flock, but he searched for it until he found it. On the flip side is the name and address of a local funeral home whose owner hopes to be remembered favorably when that time of earthly sorrow comes.

It was a hot, steamy night in July of 1954 when the humble congregation gathered to worship in the tiny church during a night of revival that would lead to a rather vocal, determined woman pushing tradition aside to have her say.

It is absolutely safe to say that back on that night in 1954, there was no air conditioning but plenty of funeral home fans moving at a rapid pace throughout the steamy church. It was the first church that my daddy had been called to pastor and though it was filled with some of the most God-loving people in the world, the community was divided between the righteous and the renegades. Moonshining was big industry in that tiny mountain county. Though there was only 3,000 residents, the county's historical archives now report that in the mid-1950s, over 50,000 gallons of moonshine was being transported *weekly* out of the county.

It actually might be fairer to say that there were more renegades than righteous residing there. A preacher at another county church would later recall his own revival around that time when so many souls had been snatched away from Satan and won for Jesus. That preacher was quite proud of the week's work. When the deacons called him and asked him to extend the revival for another week, he was even prouder. Perhaps the renegades were coming around, thought the naive country preacher. Later the truth would emerge.

The men who stealthily transported the illegal brew out of the mountains were known as moonshine runners. Cagey bunch that they were — that ol' Scotch-Irish ingenuity always available in plentiful portions to them — they realized that a revival for the righteous was just what the renegades needed. Not for the soul, mind you, but for the sake of shady enterprise.

"The Lord doth provide," remarked one of the runners with a smile years later when he retold the tale.

That week as the faithful gathered to praise and pray, the moonshine runners had parked their cars — loaded with the devil's brew — outside the church and waited for the congregants to leave. As the saints, their souls refreshed, turned on their headlights and eased out into the road, the sinners followed. Since the sheriff and his men had no reason to be suspicious of cars leaving a revival, the runners waved at them and cheerfully sailed on by. They say that more moonshine left the county that revival week than ever before or since.

It was into this kind of land that my daddy went to pastor his first church. Over twenty years later, when I was a young girl, Mama, Daddy, and I went back to visit that church on Homecoming Day, a special day set aside for all former or wayward members to return to the fold. Slowly, Daddy turned off the red dirt road and eased the car across the gravel parking area, the wheels of the car crunching softly in the gentle warmth of the spring afternoon. He parked beneath two enormous oak trees and settled back in his seat to take a look around. The small, white clapboard church was the same though a small addition for Sunday school rooms had been tacked onto the back. From the ceiling of the tiny porch hung a single naked light bulb with a dirty white string hanging down, just long enough for an adult to grab it and pull it for the light to come on.

In the backseat, I scooted forward, placed my folded arms on the front seat, and rested my chin on my hands, seeing for the first time this church about which I had heard so much. I watched as Daddy's green eyes scanned across the church yard and then stopped on the cemetery in the back of the building. Though I was only twelve, I knew him well enough to know that his mind was traveling back in time, flipping through scenes from those days passed.

Staring at the graves, he shook his head quietly. "I buried more men in that graveyard that died with their shoes on than died with 'em off."

The statement startled me so much that I jerked my head up. "What! What are you talkin' about? What do you mean 'died with their shoes on'?"

He turned his solemn eyes toward me, tinged with the memorable sadness of those lonesome, solemn journeys to bury the dead in their simple, pine caskets. There was almost always a widow left behind and, usually, a pack of young'uns who, from that day forward, would seldom know from where would come their next meal. Steadily, he gazed directly into my eyes as he answered. "That means that most of 'em were killed. Murdered. Usually shot down in a dispute over illegal whiskey."

I had been born late in life to my parents — a change-of-life baby as they called it back then — so those unsettling years of his early ministry were something of which I knew nothing. But it sure sounded interesting so I wanted to know more. I pleaded for details. It was then that Daddy, a spellbinding storyteller, would tell me the story of that night, of one boy's journey into relentless darkness and the defiant woman who would battle valiantly to draw her family into the light.

Occasionally, the renegades joined the righteous in church, probably more out of curiosity than a yearning for salvation. Daddy, never a longwinded preacher, was nearly through with his evening revival sermon when the front door banged open and four teenage boys—all sons of rebellious renegades—clattered in noisily and plopped down loudly on the back bench. The preacher stopped for a moment, eyed them steadily with disapproval for their blatant disrespect, then picked up the thread of his sermon. He started to weave it toward a finish, making a plea for salvation for any of whom might want to be washed by the blood of the Lamb. As the church folks sang "Softly and Tenderly," one of the more poignant altar-call songs, he stepped down from the pulpit and walked halfway down the short aisle.

"If you don't know the Lord Jesus Christ as your Savior, don't hesitate," he intoned. "Come to the Lord today. We have no promise of tomorrow. No guarantee that we'll live to see another day."

The boys—self-proclaimed sinners and rightly proud of it— laughed loudly, smacked chewing gum, and talked among themselves. The smell of whiskey that drenched them thoroughly permeated the church, its stench intensified by the sweltering heat. Still, the preacher stood tall for the Lord, trying to stare down the devil's disciples, but it was to no avail. Before the call for salvation ended, they all stumbled drunkenly out the door and on their way for a date with destiny.

If it had happened a couple of miles closer and a few minutes later, then those who had been in the congregation would have heard it as they lingered in the church yard to fellowship and talk as the children chased fireflies in the moonlit night. They surely would have heard the screeching tires and the exploding sheet metal as the car in which the four boys were traveling, missed a curve at a high rate of speed and bounced in midair from one tree to another. When the car finally quit rolling at the bottom of the steep embankment, it was twisted and tangled into a mess of not much left at all while the lives of each boy — not a one of them over nineteen — expired in a haze of whiskey, smoking sheet metal, and complete darkness.

The young preacher had been right. There would be no tomorrow for any of those boys.

"The saddest thing a preacher will ever do is stand and preach the funeral of a man he thinks has died without a hope in God," Daddy recounted, tears filling his eyes as he looked toward the unkempt grave of one of those boys. Two decades had drifted by, but the scars of that night remained planted on a man's heart, still tender — too tender — to the touch of the memory.

Incredibly, the worse was yet to come.

As Daddy stood with broken heart and open Bible over the lifeless body of a young man who, only two days earlier, had mocked the very altar on which he now lay, he was startled to hear a thundering commotion in the back of the church. The door flung open, banging against the dingy painted wall, and there in the doorway, covering most of the sunlight with her considerable girth, was the boy's aunt, his daddy's sister.

My father knew her well. She was one of the most faithful members of the church, a woman devoted completely to the Lord she loved. If there had ever been a better example of the chasm that divided a family between righteous and rebellious than the family from which she came, no one had ever seen it. The doors of the church were never open that she did not enter it, while her brother and his family never darkened the doors of the church.

She was quite a sight to behold, standing there in the door. To her enormous bosom she clutched a worn, tattered Bible. A harrowing take-no-prisoners kind of look was embedded deeply in her eyes, while anger tightened her pale lips into a hard pout. She took a determined breath then marched toward the casket, her sensible, low-heeled shoes pounding hard on the creaky wood floor with every step. The sound reverberated like angry thunder on a peaceful summer's day while not even a finger moved among those seated in the pews.

Daddy knew that look. It meant no good was storming down that aisle. The one thing he had come to expect from these unusual, stubborn people was the unexpected.

"*Quariest* folks you ever saw," he said, using an old Scotch-Irish term for odd. "Some of the best people, too, I ever knowed, but they were set in their ways. No denying that. They did just as they dog-goned pleased. On that you could always count."

But no one was prepared for what happened next.

The aunt stormed straight toward the casket where her nephew lay in repose, his hands folded across his chest. When she got there, she raised her right hand; then with all the force made possible by her imposing size, she dropped it furiously. As her hand met the cold, stiff cheek of her brother's son, the sickening sound of the self-righteous smack echoed throughout the church. Those who were there that day and heard it would never forget the sound of that slap for it was something they had never heard before and, good Lord willing, would never hear again.

"I didn't know what to do," Daddy recalled. "I just stepped down from the pulpit to the head of the casket and motioned to the undertaker. Not that I knew what we'd do when he got there."

Her nostrils flaring with the anger that seized her body, she took another deep breath as she stared for a second at the dead boy. Then, still clutching the Bible to her bosom, she wheeled around to face the congregation, many of whom she worshiped with every time the church doors opened. Once again, the unexpected reared its head when, like ice melting in the harsh July sun, her anger dissolved to anguish. Tears rushed down her cheeks as she prepared to have her say.

"I'll tell yu'uns what this preacher won't tell yu'uns." She flung a finger toward the deceased. "This boy has *died* and *gone* to *hell*." Dramatically, she placed a heavy emphasis on the most important words in that sentence as a collective gasp of disbelief spread across the pews. She lifted her chin, pulled back her shoulders, and turned to face her brother, his wife, and their other sons. "And it's where the rest of yu'uns is goin' too if yu'uns don't change your ways." She wiped the tears from her cheek with the back of her hand, sniffed hard, and continued, her voice quivering with agony. "I've *prayed* for ya, I've *cried* for ya, and I've *begged* ya to come to church and change your Godless ways, but you paid me no mind. Now, it's too late for this boy, and it'll be too late for the rest of yu'uns." She punctuated the remark with a firm nod of her head.

Her piece said, she took herself and her Bible and marched back up the aisle and out of the door of the church, leaving behind a tale that would become more than just mountain lore. It would become legend.

A bit later, in that simple cemetery behind that simple church, they lowered a plain pinewood box into a six-foot-deep hand-dug grave and then covered it with red Georgia clay. They laid him not to rest, mind you, for none of them believed that that boy would ever know peace and rest. They simply buried him as best they knew how, with a Scripture of some kind, a few verses of a song, and a prayer by the young preacher that called on God Almighty to send, somehow, peace and comfort to those in despair. He counted himself among those desperate for comfort of some kind. Daddy shook hands with the grief-stricken family, offered his words of condolences, and, heart-broken even further over what had transpired in the church, turned to walk across the rocky, uneven ground, carefully sidestepping other graves as he went.

"Hey Preacher!" he heard someone call and turned to see the dead boy's brother rushing to catch up with him. "Kin ya wait up a minute?"

Daddy stopped and waited, watching the thin, gaunt boy of twenty or twenty-one, take long strides toward him. He was dressed plainly in cotton work pants, a plaid shirt, and a brimmed hat plopped to an angle. He drew up close to the preacher, respectfully removed his hat, and nervously fingered the brim as he cleared his throat. His eyes cast toward the ground, he choked out his words. "Preacher, will ya pray for me?" Before Daddy could answer, the boy raised his eyes, as tears spilled down his cheek. "I need 'cha to pray." His next words were halting but earnest. "'Cause I wanna go," he stopped to swallow hard, "where I know my brother ain't."

I think it would be impossible for me to hear words stronger or more pitiful than those—"I wanna go where I know my brother ain't."

While today's sophistication and civility makes this story from over a half century ago seem archaic and primitive, it happened. Fact, as they say, is often stranger and more powerful than fiction.

Many things move me about this story, but something I particularly marvel at is that this woman, strong in her Christian convictions, did not shrink back at a time when women, like children, were expected to be seen and not heard. As the heart of the body of Christ, she had shown tough love, reminding those she loved that choices have consequences. Tough love, the kind that sees the big picture, is hard to practice, but sometimes it is the most important love we will ever give in this life.

The episode marked a turning point for that young preacher and that church. The righteous became a bit more tolerant, and the renegades became a bit less defiant. There was a gradual melting of obstinate pride that blended together the two sides, and the next summer, the young preacher baptized twenty-eight on one Sunday in the nearby river. From the ashes of despair and destruction, hope had been resurrected.

Women are of great importance to the life of a church and to the body of Christ. No church can stand and prosper emotionally and spiritually without a strong group of women who pray, teach, sing, play the piano, and cook. Besides, in all my years of church participation, I have never known one man to make a casserole for a church supper or wash the dishes afterwards.

Chapter 21

THE LORD BE WITH YOU 'TIL WE MEET AGAIN

*N*ewly graduated from college, I was eager to be off and about my own business of growing up. Over the next few years, I would chase adventure in alien cities—those of the North—and have life smack me around from time to time.

Days before I was to pack up and leave for Washington, D.C., for a sports-writing job, Mama and I lunched together in an old diner downtown, the kind with red leather booths and large plate-glass windows. Mama poured cream in her coffee and cleared her throat.

Here it comes, I thought, chewing on a French fry. *The big advice.* And it was.

"I've done my best to raise you right," she began. "And there ain't no doubt that you know right from wrong. So I just have one thing to say to you." She raised her eyes from the coffee, looked at me directly, and pointed that slightly crooked forefinger. "Forget not to assemble thyself in the house of the Lord." She paused for effect because Mama, like all of my people, was nothing short of dramatic. Like many of her generation, she spoke lyrically, often in the words of King James.

"That's the same thing my mama told me when I left home, and it's still good advice after all these years."

Well, I didn't forget. I just didn't. Most of the time, that is. In those first few years of my foray into grown-up young adulthood, I was arrogant, self-absorbed, and mildly defiant. After laying claim to twelve straight years of Sunday school awards for perfect attendance, I chose to sleep late on Sundays, visit museums, or just loll about in my pajamas, leisurely drinking coffee and watching old black-and-white movies. I paid a price for that rebellion, for peace was not a close friend of mine in those days. I was restless and always searching for a better boyfriend, a prettier dress, or a job that would make me happier.

Somehow I stumbled my way back into the fold and into a church pew regularly on Sunday mornings. The Bible after all does say, "Train up a child in the way he should go and when he is *old*, he will not depart from it."

When I returned to the discipline of worshiping God in congregation and reading my Bible daily, I discovered that God was right where I left him. He had not moved. I had.

It is truly a peace that surpasses all understanding when you walk close in the Lord's fold and hold tightly to the mighty hand. There are times that I still stumble, but thanks to the grasp he has on my hand, I do not fall. Jesus promised in the book of John, "Nothing shall pluck you from my hand."

Yes, there was a time it bothered me that the little old ladies on the first few pews seemed to always know my comings and goings and if I was down with the flu. In my impetuous youth, I proclaimed it to be downright nosy. In my enlightened later years, I pronounce it to be compassionate and loving. What bogged me down then, now lifts me up.

I really can't recall ever missing church when I was young. I don't remember ever being sick enough that it gave me a free pass to stay at home in the bed while the redeemed gathered to worship the Almighty. I do remember *trying* to get Daddy to let me stay home with some minor sore throat or stomach upset, and I remember the story he always, without fail, would recount.

"Remember what Miss Eula said," he began, and as soon as I heard that, I knew I might as well march myself to my room and put on my Sunday clothes.

Miss Eula was already ancient when I first met her and Daddy was called to pastor her church. Her husband, John, had been one of the guiding forces of the little church, though he was long dead when we came along. His sweet, saintly wife, Eula, was about four-foot-eleven, slightly bent in her posture, which made her appear even tinier. I remember her clearly, in simple print cotton dresses, often belted, a little hat, sensible black shoes, and her big black pocketbook always tucked into the crook of her arm. One Sunday, her arthritis was acting up mightily, but the precious woman, somewhere in her eighties at that point, still showed up for church. She never missed. Daddy always waited at the front door of the church and shook every adult hand and patted every child's head as the congregation dispersed when church was over. When Miss Eula offered her frail, gnarled hand that Sunday, Daddy said, "Miss Eula, how are you doin' today?"

She smiled through her pain and weakly replied, "Well, I ain't doin' so good, preacher. My ol' arthritis is actin' up something fierce, and I can barely move."

Gently, Daddy patted her on the shoulder. "Well, I sure do hate to hear that, but we're mighty glad to have you here today. We wouldn't have blamed you a bit, though, if you'd had to stay home."

She shook her head firmly, and the flowers on her little hat bounced joyfully. "No, preacher, I ain't stayin' home. I kin have my

WHAT SOUTHERN WOMEN KNOW ABOUT FAITH

aches and pains in the House of the Lord just as good as I kin have 'em at home."

From that day forward, my daddy repeated that story often from the pulpit and at home, faithfully reciting her words as though they had leaped from the lips of one of the prophets. Needless to say, if ailing Miss Eula could make it to church, then a robust child had no excuses at all.

So there were times I was forced into the pews and many times when I sat there mindlessly during one of Daddy's sermons, day-dreaming of various things, like the cute boy in my English class or my recreational plans for the afternoon. What I would give to be able to go back in time and listen to every word that had proceeded from the mouth of that dear, wise man. It amazes me but somehow some of his words managed to squeeze past the daydreams and trespass into my closed mind.

Whenever I read the Bible and come upon words from Jesus that begin with "verily, verily," I can clearly hear Daddy preaching, "Now pay close attention when it says 'verily, verily,' before Jesus speaks. That means it's very important and Jesus was tellin' everyone to listen closely to what he was about to say."

On another occasion, I remember him preaching about Solomon and the two mothers who had argued over whose baby it was. Solomon had commanded that the baby be cut in half and shared between them, knowing that the real mother would never allow that and that she would step aside to save her baby's life. Then, he would know which was the true mother.

"Solomon was the wisest man this world has ever knowed," he intoned. "For he prayed not for wealth or power or fame. He prayed for wisdom." Here, I can see Daddy stopping for effect and looking around the congregation. "For he knew that if he had wisdom, every-thing else would come to him — wealth, power, and fame."

How many times I've prayed specifically for money to help me out of a jam or divine intervention for similar material requests, I can-not count. Had I listened to my daddy's words and prayed for wisdom instead, I'd be far better off than I am today. I certainly wouldn't have made some of the foolish decisions that I have made.

I can hear some of his other oft-repeated words, gleaned from the pages of the Bible:

"For what is a man profited, if he shall gain the whole world, and lose his own soul?"

"It is easier for a camel to go through the eye of a needle, than for a rich man to enter into the kingdom of God."

"The truth shall make you free."

He was a disciple of faith, practicing what he preached. The Bible says that each believer receives one or more spiritual gifts, such as discernment, knowledge, wisdom, healing, and so on. Daddy had the gift of faith, more than anyone I've ever known. Faith — believing in an unseen power and its ability to do anything impossible for man to do — came easily and without second thought for Daddy. He prayed, left it in the Lord's hands, and then went on his way until the Lord answered.

I have never forgotten a story he told once when I was about thir-teen or fourteen. He was preaching on the Scripture that says you can pray for a mountain to be moved and it shall, if you have the tiniest amount of faith, the size of an itty bitty mustard seed.

"Don't be like the old woman who got down on her knees and prayed and prayed for a mountain to be moved," he warned. "She prayed for two days and when she got up and looked out her window, she saw that the mountain was still there. 'See there, God,' she said, 'I knowed you wouldn't move that mountain!'"

I've been guilty of that. I've prayed, and when it didn't happen, I too have said, "I didn't figure it would." And each time, I have thought back to Daddy's sermon that day. I can remember it clearly, him standing tall, broad-shouldered, handsome, and well-dressed in a dark suit and conservative tie. When he walked away from the pulpit so that the lectern did not separate him from the congregation, he would always carry his black Bible in his hand, with his fingers sprawled wide, holding the Bible open.

Many teachings pressed upon me in my carefree youth have somehow managed to stick with me. All of my Bibles are black, going back to Daddy's preference for that color and how he always proclaimed, "Out of the darkness came the light. Bibles oughta be black because from the dark cover comes the light."

"Never lay anything on top of the Word of God," he would scold severely if I had unthinkingly laid a magazine on top of his Bible.

To this day, a Bible in my house never has anything on top of it.

As I've grown older, I've realized that the teachings of my childhood are the anchor of my adult life. While I paid little attention to them at the time, somehow those teachings and ancient truths engulfed my being, and when I was mature enough, they rose up to guide my life. Though I have no children of my own, I understand clearly now that it is important that children be raised in Sunday school and church. Just as surely as the calcium in milk will make their bones strong for a lifetime, nutrition received early from the Holy Spirit will make them emotionally and spiritually strong for life. Even if they don't seem to be listening to the sermons.

"God be with you till we meet again," I often heard preachers say as they closed out a service. I can close my eyes and hear my daddy's sweet, humble voice closing a sermon by whispering, "May God rest his mighty hand on your shoulder until it tears his purpose for us to meet again."

Now, there are many who have gone on before me and made that crossing over the River Jordan: Daddy, Mama, my brother, a nephew, my grandparents, cousins, uncles, aunts, beloved friends, and the first boy I ever loved, whom I loved until death called his name and, despite my woeful pleas for mercy, pulled him away for heaven's gates.

Thanks to the faithful teachings of my people and their unyielding belief in a great and loving God that trickled down and led to my own salvation, I have complete assurance that I will see each and every one again in a glorious place that is better by far than this ol' vale of tears and sorrow.

I know not the day nor the hour of that heavenly reunion. But this I know with complete confidence: God will be with me until we meet again.

ACKNOWLEDGMENTS

*I*t never ceases to amaze me how God's plan is always perfect and timely. How he can begin, years in advance, to place together the pieces of an intricate puzzle.

During the week that I began work in earnest on this book, I picked up Daddy's worn, black Bible — the one I read most mornings — and it fell open to the first chapter of Revelation. Daddy rarely marked in his Bibles, but he had highlighted one Scripture, and above it was a heading that read: The Command To Write.

It caught my attention and I read the highlighted passage, which would become the guiding instruction for this book: "Write the things which thou hast seen, and the things which are, and the things which shall be hereafter" (Revelation 1:19).

From beyond the grave, Daddy gave me the direction for this book from a Scripture that the Lord had laid on his heart many years ago, before I even had written my first book. That is what I have sought to do in the preceding pages.

Now, there are so many others to thank that it is quite possible that I will miss someone dear and regret it terribly. Still, I must take that chance.

Dudley Delffs, the dearest editor possible, conceived the idea of *What Southern Women Know about Faith*. He took it to the most amazing agent possible (and one of God's many blessings to me), Jenny Bent, who recognized the brilliance of the idea and enthusiastically brought it to me. I simply complied with their vision and set about the task as Daddy had outlined for me. To both of you: thank you from a very grateful Southern gal.

Dudley is in the most enviable position of being surrounded by a stellar group of individuals at Zondervan, who are remarkable people as well as being terrifically talented at the jobs they do. They took our work and maximized its worth. It's impossible to name each precious person who has touched this book in some way along the way but I must name the ones who were in the trenches early: Marcy Schorsch, Ginia Hairston, Karen Campbell, Joyce Ondersma, and Bob Hudson. This has been the most pleasant publishing experience that an author could possibly enjoy. Thank y'all mightily.

To the women, all of whom are family or friends, whose stories lie in these pages, I am humbled to be able to relate your experiences of grace and faith to a larger audience. Thank you for allowing me to share these stories so that other lives might be touched by the depths of your faith.

As I set out to write this book, it seemed to rain death and heartache. Finally, I discovered that it was too hard to write at home, the place where my enchanting Mama had recently breathed her last breath on this earth. Thank God for all the friends who stepped forward and offered their vacation homes as writing sanctuaries.

At least half of this book was written in the Tennessee lakeside home of Darrell and Stevie Waltrip. They had long offered the house whenever I wanted to visit, so it was an easy phone call to make because the answer was quickly, "We'd be thrilled for you to use it as long as you need it." I shall remember always the prayer that Darrell prayed over me that afternoon before he and Stevie left. He put his arms around Stevie and me, hugged us close, and prayed that God would bless my writings and let inspiration flow easily. And so it did. I wrote nonstop, feverishly. It was one of the grandest gifts I have ever been given.

There was also a week spent at my friend Kim Waters' beautiful home at the edge of the Cherokee Forest, way up in the North Georgia mountains. Again, that's always an easy phone call. I just let Kim know what I need and I have it.

Down in St. Simons Island, Georgia, I often meet the angels of inspiration. For some reason, I write exceedingly well in that wonderful little place where, when I was fifteen years old, while standing in the cemetery of Christ Church, I met the renowned writer, Eugenia Price, and made up my mind that I would write books one day. Sisters Cathy Foster and Louise Bartlett are always quick to throw open the doors to Grandma's House—the pretty little cottage left to them by their Methodist Church piano-playing grandmother—whenever I need to escape. I wrote the detailed outline for this book at the cottage, then six months later returned to finish what I had begun. Though I never knew her, I feel that Grandma is a saintly friend of mine who always welcomes me into her cottage close to the sea. Thank you to all of you who opened your homes to me. I have no doubt that God will bless you richly for your generosity.

If a family is lucky, it will have someone who will see the value in history before it *is* history and record it. I was grateful to LaWayne who, decades ago, had recorded several sermons of Daddy's. I listened to those sermons and found them to be an enormous help in returning me to his particular lilting cadence and language that was a beautiful blending of the King James Bible and the Scotch-Irish vernacular. It was an enormous help in setting the tone for many stories.

I must also make a special note of gratitude to Stevie, who stepped out of her place of comfort and, for me and our precious Lord, wrote the foreword. While she may have doubted her ability, I never did for one moment. I knew she would write beautifully and appropriately. And so she did.

I have gathered many friends along the way since I wrote my first book. I am indebted to Richard Curtis, who first saw the value in me writing about Southern women, and author friends like Dottie Benton Frank, Jill Conner Browne, Cassandra King, Susan Reinhardt, and Celia Rivenbark. They are all loyal women on whom I know I can call at any time.

To Jeff and Gregg Foxworthy, Dolly Parton, Paula Deen, Anne Rivers Siddons, Marsha Barbour, Don Light, Mary Eaddy, and Judi Turner, thank you for your kindness, help, and generosity. To Senator Zell Miller, you are a hero to many, including me. Thank you for your encouragement and inspiration.

Fervent prayers of many carried me through, and I needed them, especially after I lost the earthly prayers of Mama. Karen, Debbie, Bridget, Pinky, Nicole, Stevie, Sue, and Louise can always be counted on for a loving word, a kind encouragement, and a powerful prayer. Thanks girls!

Mary Nell proved to be a big help when Dixie Dew's babysitter up and went to heaven and I needed a loving home for a chubby dachshund when I was traveling. What a Godsend. Thank you so much.

Dear, sweet Patti and precious Brandon help me to keep things running when life is running me crazy. You both are such a blessing to me. I couldn't do it without you.

Selena, the resident photographer in our family, cheerfully brought her skills and talent to help complete this book with the author's photo we needed. Thank you, dear girl. You captured my kitchen beautifully! It doesn't even look fat.

Finally, I am grateful for parents who taught me of the Savior who bought me with his blood, to quote an old Southern gospel hymn, and a family that continues to fervently practice faith with a spirit of active worship and steadfast belief. Of all the many blessings that shower my life, the faith of my parents and family is the most precious.

To all of you who read these pages, I hope our combined efforts will bless you as much as I have been blessed along the path of this extraordinary journey. God bless us all. I pray he will.

Share Your Thoughts

With the Author: Your comments will be forwarded to the author when you send them to *zauthor@zondervan.com*.

With Zondervan: Submit your review of this book by writing to *zreview@zondervan.com*.

Free Online Resources at

www.zondervan.com

Zondervan AuthorTracker: Be notified whenever your favorite authors publish new books, go on tour, or post an update about what's happening in their lives at www.zondervan.com/authortracker.

Daily Bible Verses and Devotions: Enrich your life with daily Bible verses or devotions that help you start every morning focused on God. Visit www.zondervan.com/newsletters.

Free Email Publications: Sign up for newsletters on Christian living, academic resources, church ministry, fiction, children's resources, and more. Visit www.zondervan.com/newsletters.

Zondervan Bible Search: Find and compare Bible passages in a variety of translations at www.zondervanbiblesearch.com.

Other Benefits: Register yourself to receive online benefits like coupons and special offers, or to participate in research.

ZONDERVAN®

ZONDERVAN.com/
AUTHORTRACKER
follow your favorite authors